Some Fishes I Have Known
A Reef Rescue Odyssey

by Snorkel Bob, Himself

SKYHORSE PUBLISHING

Skyhorse Publishing books may be purchased in bulk at special discounts for sales promotion, corporate gifts, fund-raising, or educational purposes. Special editions can also be created to specifications. For details, contact the Special Sales Department, Skyhorse Publishing, 555 Eighth Avenue, Suite 903, New York, NY 10018 or info@skyhorsepublishing.com.

www.skyhorsepublishing.com

All photos by Snorkel Bob, Himself, unless otherwise noted.

10 9 8 7 6 5 4 3 2 1

Library of Congress Cataloging-in-Publication data is available on file.
ISBN: 978-1-61608-140-9

Printed in China

For Kupuna Ed Lindsey, who said, "Hawaii's fishes belong to the people of Hawaii. Taking them for amusement is an affront to Hawaiian culture."

For Papa Henry Auwae, whom I never met before he passed in 2001, but who caught my ear down the line when he said, "You don't have to be born Hawaiian to live *pono*."

And for those Hawaiians and others who try for a *pono* (right and just) way of life, especially in holding Hawaii reefs in trust and close to their hearts, including Justin Gruenstein, Rene Umberger, Ziggy Livnat, Mayor Charmaine Tavares, Senator Roz Baker and the Maui Legislative Delegation, Mike Moran and the Kihei Community Association, Rocky and Jerry Kaluhiwa, Mahealani Cypher and the Ko'olaupoko, Ko'olauloa, Waimanalo, and Kailua Hawaiian Civic Clubs, Keiko Bonk, Brooks Tagamine, Kimokeo Kapahulehua, Randy Awo, Kuhea Paracuelles, Senator Josh Green, Kecia Joy, Shirley Casuga, the Maui County Council, Uncle Buzzy Agard, Lucienne de Naie, Dale Bonar, the Maui Nui Marine Resource Council, Robin Knox, Julie Leialoha, Irene Bowie and Maui Tomorrow, Jim Coon, Pauline Feine, Kurt Fevella, Brooke Porter, Congresswoman Maize Hirono, Lance Holter and the Maui Sierra Club, Makaala Kaaumoana, Earth Justice, Michelle Anderson, Kai Nishiki, Uncle Charlie Maxwell, Marjorie Zeigler and the Conservation Council of Hawaii, Joe McDonald, MiQe, Jeff and Jody King, Nan and Neil Rhodes, Linda Paul, Tina Owens, Butch Helemano, Madge Schaeffer, Diane Shepherd, Ellyn Tong, Uncle Walter Paolo, Marti Townsend, Miwa Tamanaha and Kahea, Aka Mahi, Sara Peck, Ann Fielding, Rob Parsons, the entire staff at Snorkel Bob's, The Humane Society of the United States, Robin Newbold, Anita the Mermaid, and all who see, feel, and know the fish.
Y mucho mahalos tambien to Keith "Matt Roving" Christie and to Joan Lloyd for guidance and support.

Utmost and forevermore for King Neptune. May the reefs return to glory . . .

On board were the twelve:

The poet, the physician, the farmer, the scientist,

The magician and the other so-called Gods of our legends.

Though Gods they were—

And as the elders of our time choose to remain blind,

Let us rejoice and let us sing and dance and ring in the new . . .

Hail Atlantis!

—donovan

Some Fishes I Have Known

An old joke asks, What's the last thing that goes through a gnat's mind when he splats into your windshield? The answer: his ass.

Ha!

Get it?

Most humor is based on incongruity; by common sense standards, such a premise could not be, and in fact is so outrageous that it's laughable. Yet we take the bait, in this case the proposition that a gnat has a mind—a generator of thought, feeling, and perception. Short of getting gnats to take an IQ test, we may never measure their intellectual acuity, and so the joke will persist.

Meanwhile, a few people of the human variety, like some Hindus and snorkel executives, speculate in earnest that a growing proportion of nonhuman beings are sentient.

This concept is fundamental to a book suggesting acquaintance with a group of fish. Reef addicts who have known a sociable fish or 2 may comprehend best that some whimsy is grounded intuitively, that science can be blind, that hellbent data may disprove our own lying eyes. How many technocrats do you know who would admit to a personal relationship with a fish?

A few years ago, a roster of severely qualified scientists and I, Snorkel F.* Bob, addressed a conservation forum. My topic was aquarium collecting in Hawaii, a woeful pursuit, and I am familiar. Yet I wondered: a bunch of scientists and *moi*?

So 30 speakers with the PhD credential and a snorkel exec were to shed light on the state of Hawaii reefs. Marine scientists have traditionally measured reef health in 2 ways: the 1st by counting fish to assess species variation, decline, or growth, and the 2nd by a transect grid system sectioning a reef into 1-meter squares, so each numbered square can be evaluated for coral growth, coral damage, native and invasive algae cover, and the like.

I, Snorkel Bob, presented a 3rd column of qualitative analysis: snorkeling a reef to see its health and vibrancy. I, Snorkel Bob, am an inveterate 3rd-column practitioner, but my equal billing to all those scientists seemed to challenge the value of the PhD or any moniker. What did I do, but go snorkeling, have fun, get lucky on an opinion or 2 with a deep regard for grammar, diction, and syntax—oh, and style, not to mention flourish, and a lilting *je ne sais quoi* to playfully tease the boundaries of propriety, gaining a blush and a chortle in minimalist strokes, and repeat as necessary? That's not much, really, compared to cramming for days and all-nighters, years of primetime spent pupating in a campus cocoon with scant hope that a professor might someday emerge—meanwhile popping No Doze like M&Ms, nodding off, ears steaming, and getting it right, because failure means life in the real world.

Yet equal billing at the conservation forum indicated that vast advertising expenditure may equal advanced degrees, when it comes to authority.

Of course I, Snorkel Bob'm too humble; some advertisers spend obscenely and still can't convey concisely in the clear light of meaning, import, and amusement. A Snorkel Executive joined to his cat in holy matrimony (!), and a revolutionary, fresh-air snorkel got the headline: **Hey, Moflo!** (The Aloha Airlines in-flight publisher claimed Ebonics abuse. Can you imagine? They're out of business.) A dog caught waves on a boogie board, and myriad more milestone moments made mirthful magnitude over the years, stretching a smile across the collective face.

But back to the doctors of philosophy, most of whom spent many semesters treading the lofty ether, striving for buoyancy, reaching for flotsam if not wisdom. Some wizened matriculates retained a sense of humor. A few, awestruck by an international celebrity, spewed admiration: "Snorkel Bob! You're huge!"

Few men will casually dismiss the XXXL accolade, though the follow-up can be awkward: "How big are you?"

The response was, is, and shall be: "We're as big as Lex Brodie." Lex Brodie is Mr. Tire here in Hawaii, and he may have an original idea or 2. His ad budget is gargantuan, and our society is a tad influenced by repetitive media. Maybe he didn't get invited because old tires didn't work out so well as artificial reef material.

I, Snorkel Bob, also spent millions on ads over the years—clever ads, to be sure; did I mention a snorkel exec in drag, comparing silicone to reality! Then there's the campaign against aquarium collecting in Hawaii to our credit, plus a few other good deeds here and there. Can you imagine those guys, picking our reefs clean, legally?

My own scholarly success, however, is meager, yielding naught but a circumlocutory bent on a multifaceted reality, residual of the extracurricular, I'm sure. But the experimental phase of the college years is where curiosity plays out, forming the building blocks of the future. We are here because of youthful indiscretion and free association. What could better teach the lesson of risk? Our mixed, free-enterprise society rewards nothing more than risk. Authority goes to the winners, who win often as not by chance. A little timing, a little luck, a reasonable skill set, *et voila!* While science requires continual funding and political survival, showbiz grants authority directly. Box office returns are hard news, along with outlandish behavior and massive expenditure.

THE POINT is: authority or celebrity can run flat as new tires—or a big ad budget or an advanced degree. *Some Fishes I Have Known* is not scientific. It's a flight of fancy. (A swim of fancy? A swimsical review?) It's a record of reef communion and the New Reef Order. These pictures will entertain and enlighten, often at shallow depth. Kimokeo Kapahulehua assures me: The fish see. The fish feel. The fish know.

The fish know? What does a fish know?

What does anybody know? You're born. You live. You die. You spend years in school. Some days you're dull, lost in numbing indifference. On the bright side, sometimes you're on—on message, on point, on your game, delivering with timing and style.

Some people are blessed with times of meaning and play—but enough of philosophy; no course credit here. I'll end on a formal endorsement of informal education practically applied with the God-given gifts enabling 3rd column research. At the U. of Reefs we don't call a fish by its Latin binomial, or measure the ratio of its anterior fins to its posterior margins. We do not examine the contents of 19 specimens or count the rows or numbers of back teeth. How do they do those things? Do they put the fish in little dental chairs and entice them to open wide? Do they take MRIs of these fish?

No, they don't. The fish are deemed expendable, deferential to the needs of science, or, rather, to fulfillment of grant objectives through data collection. Hey, I'm not complaining. I'm only delineating the other school of thought—and behavior.

I'm only pointing out that the 3rd column may expand a hitherto narrow perspective.

Herein are art, life, and magic. Here are 3rd column data proving that sunbeams dance and dapple the coral heads, where fish come out to see who showed up and perhaps hint at what a scaly gillbreather might perceive and feel and know.

*Frankly.

Yours in the bond,

Snorkel Bob, Himself

Snorkel Bob, Himself

In the Nursery

It's early morning on Maui's north shore, and we're motivated by a woman who may have been at the Fillmore West in that orbital season of '69, when reality got remodeled after a cosmic rhythm and original vibration. She'd seen the elusive Hawaiian seahorse, she said, about 10" long, drifting past, curling its tail around her pinky for a bonding session reminiscent of the golden era when all women were sisters, all men the same. After searching the area 2 hours, I, Snorkel Bob, wondered if the tiny steed had asked, "Are you my mama?" Like when Led Zeppelin II blasted out the hi-fi in that very same year, and the lyrics emerged in talk bubbles, so you could read them but couldn't sing along, because your vocal chords were numb to cerebral synapse, on account of . . .

Healthy coral clusters indicate growth and water quality.

Hey, look: who's complaining? Sunrise on a reef with friends and an elusive grail in our collective consciousness is a bell ringer at any age. Isn't it? Discoveries abounded just off the Waihe'e Preserve, where natural jetties bound the reef on both sides. The shallows vary in depth from 9–18", so a snorkeler who navigates poorly or drafts too deep can run aground, bruising the fragile polyps just below.

Or worse, suffer venomous dorsal spines.

The Hawaiian lionfish was commonly seen only a few years ago. Decimated by the aquarium trade and poor water quality, sightings are now rare. This baby is not relaxed—spines out. Sea creatures with venomous spines or stingers present passive danger, wounding only aggressors; respectful distance avoids injury. NOTE the flecks in the water, indicating a prolific nursery rich in plankton snax.

Hawaiian lionfish, back view (above) and side view (below).

A Hawaiian lionfish in about 14" of water at the Waihe'e Preserve on Maui's north shore, with a surge and short chop.

This was a challenge in rocky, shallow water with a heavy camera and a juvenile lionfish ready to use his dorsal spines. But these shots capture the nursery character of the place, with its abundant food source, plentiful habitat, and lack of predators. The penetrating sunlight stimulates the plankton and vegetation, which in turn make for contented baby fish.

The most striking characteristic of a nursery, however, is the presence of old familiars in perfect miniature. Now more than ever before do the young of species other than our own give hope for a reasonable future.

photo by Anita

This juvie humuhumulei *or lei triggerfish (below) is about 1½" long—she'll grow to 8–10".*

9

Which isn't to say that all fish babies are small-scale versions of adult fish. Many are not, like the yellowtail coris or the belted wrasse shown a few pages down the road. Many species are so different in the juvenile phase that they may be taken for adults of a different species. At any rate, the *humuhumulei* (or lei triggerfish) juvenile shown here in perfect proportion to the adult of the same species and coloration, gives hope that in a world of struggling reefs, the fish have not yet surrendered. Energetic babies beyond the tiny stage, with clean skin and apparent success in feeding and fitting into reef habitat, can warm the cockles of a snorkel curmudgeon's heart.

I, Snorkel Bob, could give up hope on any given day without the assurance that the game is not yet lost.

Ornate butterflyfish in the 25¢ size (left)—note the blunt body and baby face, sunbeams and sustenance abounding.

Manini is Hawaiian for small or trifling. Manini is also the common name of the convict tang (below), another surgeonfish—vital herbivores who keep reef algae in check. This fry could cover a dime if he inhaled. NOTE: Surgeonfish are so called because of a razor sharp scalpel (get it?) on either side of the caudal peduncle—the narrow section between body and tail (caudal fin). The scalpel is defensive; a tail swish cuts advances from the rear deemed, as they say, inappropriate.

This basin is still a nursery at 5–6' deep, too shallow for predator comfort (though they may cruise through), yet perfect for juvenile reef fish. The surge and short chop are far easier for a snorkeler with a little water under his keel. Sunbeams refracting in the blue keep optimism high for a seahorse sighting. The place feels like seahorse habitat. Hardly proficient swimmers but adept at moving from one tail hitch to another, seahorses need the right diameter, density, and shape of hitching posts. The Waihe'e Preserve has it all—or feels like it does, giving the urgent indication that they're right out front swaying in the surge, just out of focus.

A manini illustrates this nursery in all its benefits.

This baby belted wrasse is about 2" long.

So you stare and squint and really, really want to see the elusive Hawaiian seahorse, until a morphing marine Rorschach recalls a troubled youth and psychiatric needs, balanced only by Tuffy the dog, tail wagging like a metronome timed to the surge and pull of life itself, his tongue lapping like little waves . . . till time and tide find ethereal rhythm, so you ease up and let go of wanting, as sooner or later you must, because you can't always get what you want. Oh, no, you can't always get what you want, but if you try sometime, you just might find, you get what you need . . .

Ahhh . . .

Aahhhahhhhahhh . . .

You get what you nee-eed . . . Ahhhahhhahhhh . . .

And there before us on a morning in Waihe'e is a fish bathed in light and bound for greatness on the Wheel of Life, if not on this spin, then the next. See the balance, the fluid meditation, the inner and outer light to inform a snorkeler seeking truth on what a fish might know.

We didn't meet the Hawaiian seahorse that day. We had to settle for . . .

. . . the next Dalai Lama.

The night gave birth

Born was Kumulipo in the night, a male

Born was Po'ele in the night, a female

Born was the coral polyp, born was the coral, came forth

Born was the grub that digs and heaps up the earth, came forth

Born was his [child] an earthworm, came forth

Born was the starfish, his child the small starfish came forth

Born was the sea cucumber, his child the small sea cucumber came forth

Born was the sea urchin [tribe]

Born was the short-spiked sea urchin, came forth

Born was the smooth sea urchin, his child the long-spiked came forth

Born was the ring-shaped sea urchin, his child the thin-spiked came forth

Born was the barnacle, his child the pearl oyster came forth

Born was the mother-of-pearl, his child the oyster came forth

Born was the mussel, his child the hermit crab came forth

Born was the big limpet, his child the small limpet came forth

Born was the cowry, his child the small cowry came forth

Born was the naka shellfish, the rock oyster his child came forth

Born was the drupa shellfish, his child the bitter white shellfish came forth

Born was the conch shell, his child the small conch shell came forth

Born was the nerita shellfish, the sand-burrowing shellfish his child came forth

Born was the fresh water shellfish, his child the small fresh water shellfish came forth

Born was man for the narrow stream, the woman for the broad stream

Born was the Ekaha moss living in the sea

Guarded by the Ekahakaha fern living on land

Darkness slips into light

Earth and water are the food of the plant

The god enters, man cannot enter

Man for the narrow stream, woman for the broad stream

Born was the tough seagrass living in the sea

Guarded by the tough landgrass living on land

—Lines 12–42, Chapter 10, "Birth of Sea and Land Life" of *The Kumulipo*,
this version from www.sacred-texts.com

"Kumulipo was the husband, Po'ele the wife. To them was born Pouliuli. This was the beginning of the earth. The coral was the first stone in the foundation of the earth mentioned in the chant."

Speaking of Juveniles

All species incur infant mortality. The odds on a reef fish maturing to reproductive age are probably greater than those of insects but less than those of humans. When juvenile reef fish appear in greater numbers, hope springs anew on reef recovery, though more little fish may indicate only seasonal recruitment.

That's what we hear from scientists employed by the State of Hawaii—what we heard on Maui in the 1st, 2nd, and 3rd years following Maui's total ban on gill nets, that even though more juveniles were seen, they would dissipate to the predatory hierarchy in no time. Yet some species of Maui reef fish remain more visibly populous than prior to the gill net ban, and some reefs, especially along Maui's west and south shores, are now home to a handful of yellow tangs. That might sound like small potatoes, but reefs across Hawaii went from hundreds or thousands of yellow tangs down to zero in a relatively short time, say 20–30 years. A vocal few culprits cried foul on any effort to stop the carnage, or safeguard the reef, or quell the grab-ass, free-for-all common to resource "management" in Hawaii for decades. Maui is the most progressive island in Hawaii on conservation and has the only total ban on gill nets in Hawaii, so the first signs of species recovery are monumental.

Gill nets kill thousands of reef fish daily. Aquarium collectors often take what's left. Does this seem like management? Don't get me, Snorkel Bob, started. Suffice to say, the babies—the juvies, the recruits, the fry—give us hope that recovery to an abundance of fish is still possible. Sustainable? Around here, that word often means continuing minimum—unlimited extraction but for the last handful of brood fish, who can spawn for another

massive harvest. But the tide is turning on hope sustained, as long as reefs can host blessed events.

It all starts the same: primordial soup. Though some marine species have live birth of perfectly formed fry, most hatch from eggs that are either spawned in clusters—where they remain as the embryos develop—or cast into the flow to meet spermatozoa of the same species, which isn't so random if the egg and sperm spew in proximity to each other for likely communion and fertilization. The preceding page shows very small plankton, but hardly the smallest. A classic example of genetic programming in 2 species seemingly identical at the outset is the case of the giant squid, who can grow to 50' in 2 years, and the oval squid, fully grown in the same time to 7". Yet these 2 squid species are nearly identical as spawn.

Meanwhile, back in Hawaii, nothing brings out the sappy sentiment in a snorkel exec like baby tangs—yellow tangs, that is, the little lights that shine, reef gold, herbivores, algae eaters, gems in the coral crown.

A brand new baby tang's ribs stick out, and so do its dorsal and anal fins. The perfect habitat for yellow tangs is finger coral, endemic to Hawaii. Yellow tang captive breeding has succeeded to the point of hatching fry, but not beyond. The tiny fry have tinier mouths in need of food that's tinier still. Though success has loomed near on a diet of copepods—microplanktonic crustaceans—the exact formula is still elusive, underscoring the mystical balance of our reefs.

The aquarium industry values small fish; they fit more neatly in small tanks, and the smaller the tank, the bigger the market. Shipping live fish is tricky, however, because a fish too has to pee—*and* make #2, which fouls the cup of water in the plastic bag, which kills the fish—and the profit. The industry solution is to starve the fish prior to shipping, which also kills fish, but not as many. What's the greater solution? Perhaps it was first offered by our beloved President Ronald Reagan:

"Mr. Gorbachev, tear *down* this aquarium!"

Juvie tangs prefer finger coral, or any coral that provides quick cover from predators. Aquarium collectors are shown harvesting—pounding the finger coral with billy clubs—in the Hawaii Audubon short DVD bemoaning the practice, which is illegal, but in Hawaii enforcement is simply not practical. Another favored harvesting technique focuses on a yellow tang behavior occurring at dusk, in transition from shallow grazing to deeper slumbers. On the way they congregate in columns over the slumber zone in a social contact perhaps assuring one thing and another. Said one Maui aquarium collector, "I can drop my net down one side of that column and bring it up on the other with 400 tangs. It's a beautiful thing." What's the solution? (All together now): "Mr. Gorbachev, tear *down* this aquarium!"

This juvie yellow tang (below) is more developed than a brand new baby. Note the ribs, not so protruding. Also note the habitat here: healthy finger coral in the foreground and live rock just behind, with a moderate coating of organisms. This reef looks and is healthy, though the shoreline above it, undeveloped for several million years, was prepped for the construction of 140 faaabulous condominia in the 4 to 15.5 range. Million dollar, that is, which should have warranted safeguards of the reef out front, but of course that luxury was just too darn expensive. Then came the Great Recession. I, Snorkel Bob, love it when a grandiose developer goes belly up, instead of the fish.

By the way, the Hawaii Department of Land and Natural Resources was formed in 1956 with a mandate and mission statement to manage fisheries. DLNR took 25 years to regulate removal of coral and live rock from Hawaii reefs—i.e., removal went unchecked for 25 years as a "fishery," supporting the aquarium industry. Taking coral or live rock from Hawaii reefs is now 100% illegal. Hawaii tropical fish, however, with DLNR nearly 60 years old, have no protection, regulation, bag limit, or any form of "management." It's *carte blanche* stripping and voiding of the earth's reef system. What can we do? Did I mention Ronald Reagan?

"Mr. Gorbachev, tear *down* this aquarium!"

Easily mistaken for young yellow tangs are these juvenile orangestripe surgeonfish (inset). Note the dorsal fin running the length of the body, without the dramatic arch of the yellow tang. Also note the shape of the head: more rounded, without the pointy snout. These babies have not yet developed the scalpel on each side of the caudal peduncle, so their only defense is ducking into the coral cover.

In time, they look like this adult orangestripe surgeonfish (above). Note the dark gray scalpel on the caudal peduncle. It's not countershaded or highlighted as on many surgeons, but formidable nonetheless.

23

Here's a kick in the shorts: To the left is a chevron tang, also known as a juvenile black tang, since it will darken dramatically with maturity. Chevrons are extremely rare on the reef, but you can find them online for $150 EACH. 99% die within a year of captivity, sending the aquarium scourge deeper for more money.

Below is a young milletseed butterflyfish, so named for Neptune's sprinkling of millet seeds on its flanks.

These very small convict tangs—so called for their jailhouse jammies—snatch plankton snax and graze on shag algae alongside a junior orangestripe surgeon and 2 more juvies their parents would not likely approve of.

Hawaii is 20 degrees above the equator, while Tahiti is 17 degrees below. The math here is easy, since we know the earth is 25,000 miles in circumference, *mas o menos,* so pole to pole is about half that, or 12,500 miles covering 180 degrees, which makes each degree worth about 60 miles. Kauai is a few degrees from Kona. Ni'ihau and the Northwestern Hawaiian Islands are farther apart than that, and French Polynesia spans vast ocean realms in island clusters from the Marquesas to the north to the Society Islands to the south. So the distances are considerable.

But juveniles of many species tend to be similar around the world. This looks like a juvie milletseed butterfly, but with no black on the caudal peduncle. It's actually a citron butterfly grazing on a fuzzy rock at the point separating Opanohu and Cook's Bays, in a beach park on Moorea (right). NOTE: Opanohu beach park is now dead. Gone in 15 months.

Likewise, these youthful eels could be from the same reef but are not. They live 3,000 miles apart, above and below the equator. Both are adolescent with developing values and tastes. The snowflake on the right is setting out from a Tahiti reef, while the whitemouth moray on the left is in Hawaii. The Hawaii teen eel may be more likely to put a decal on his pickup proclaiming **Born and Raised**, but probably won't.

That is, all teens are prone to pratfall, but reef teens are more focused on personal survival, yielding only to the good of the species. Reef evolution chooses the fittest to procreate, unlike what we see off the reef.

But in all species, on and off the reef, children of a similar stripe can and do differ as adults. Take the chromis, a family of the damselfish species. In Hawaii, many reefs are decimated by gill nets, aquarium collectors, acidification, runoff, siltation,

and shoreline development. However, those reefs may still host schools of chromis, maybe an inch or 2 full grown in rich shades of brownish gray, or maybe it's grayish brown, with a dash of magenta, a hint of violet, and a smidge of aqua piping.

The chromis common to French Polynesia, on the Southern hand, is dazzling blue, or turquoise or emerald, with fish of these variant colors often integrated on the same coral head. They take deep cover into the coral nooks and crannies on the approach of a snorkeler, but then ease on out if the snorkeler can be still and drift like flotsam. Tahiti shallow waters often match the chromis in azure pastels, so that the fish are easily visible with a coral backdrop but then disappear upon rising into the water column. But I digress; the notable similarity in the Hawaii and Tahiti species is an adaptation to place by way of color, to better blend. Tahiti chromis are brightly lit in dazzling pastels, while Hawaii chromis opt for subtlety in gray, brown, and reddish tint. The difference is lost on the fry; both species show up brightly lit as juveniles, as if innately bent for truth and showbiz.

These hatchlings grow up fast, and so would you at this level of flamboyance—and snack size too.

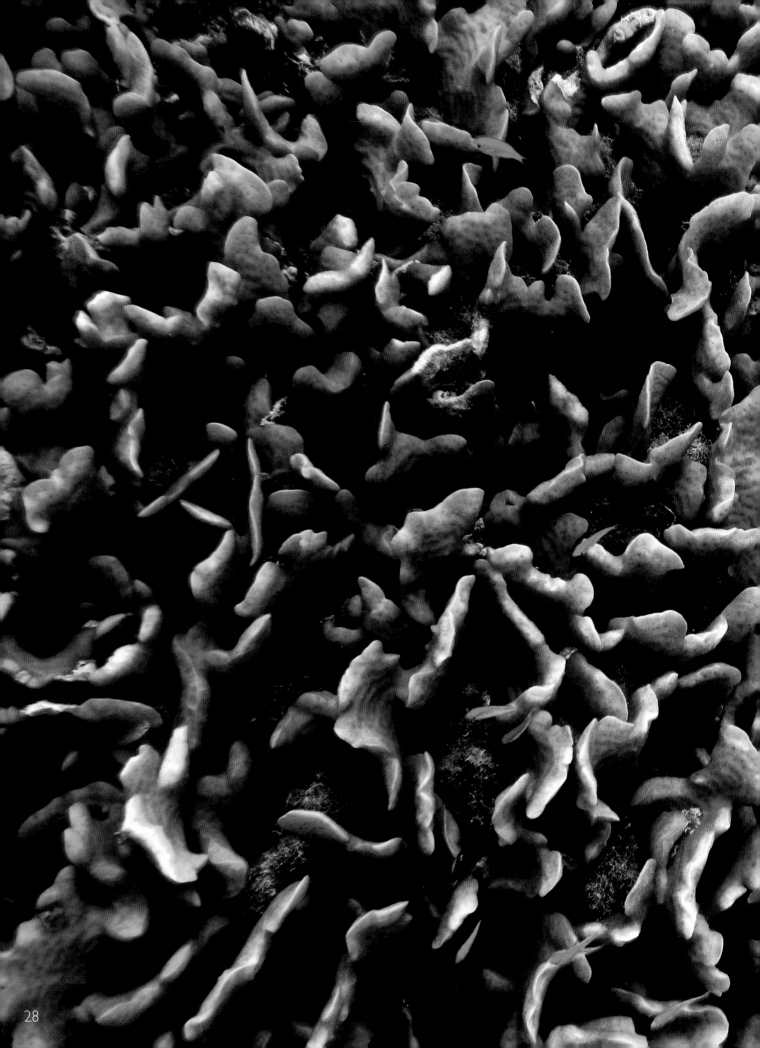

Tahiti juvenile turquoise chromis (above) and Hawaii juvenile oval chromis (inset).

29

Chromis are in the damsel family, which includes the Hawaiian dascyllus (left)—what most people call the domino fish in Hawaii. These fish also live, work, and play near a central coral head, taking cover quickly at the approach of anything huge, say 12" or better.

Isolated small corals on sandy bottoms often host a juvenile or 2 in the ¼–½" range. NOTE: If you go snake-eyed on the lower left corner of the photo you'll see a juvenile arceye hawkfish perched discreetly, hidden from the occasional predator yet ready to feed on something smaller. One day he may perch at the top of the coral head, fearless and hungry—well, with less fear, anyway.

For that matter, no juvenile wants to be too far from cover, what with predators lurking, both natural and unnatural, like those guys on MSNBC, who make contact on the internet, seeking clandestine encounter, only to wind up in a national broadcast without the discreet interlude they'd hoped for—but don't get me started, except of course to recall our Spiritual Guide of the 1980s, our President (of the United States of America) who stood tall and wouldn't run, because these colors don't, and told that pesky Russkie,

"Mr. Gorbachev, tear *down* this aquarium!"

Where was I, Snorkel Bob? Oh, yeah, on the reef with some fish children, among whom are a select few with the wits to heed their parents' warnings, that decent cover is key to survival, like these 2 shortnose wrasses. Above is a juvenile, looking too cool for school, headed this way and that, BUT not far from cover.

Below is a mature adult transitioned to a male and obviously seasoned with reef smarts.

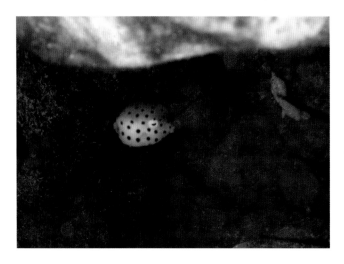

This very young boxfish is hiding under a ledge that's actually a harborside walkway fronted by big rocks. This baby has a nursery staked out where it can be safe from predators, feed on passing snax, and watch the world go by (Huahine, Tahiti).

Also keeping close to cover, a multiband butterflyfish young'un (below).

Blacklip butterflyfish showed up on Maui in late summer by the thousands upon thousands. Looks like a milletseed butterfly who's been moonlighting as a chimney sweep.

It's a young psychedelic wrasse (above), and a baby frogfish (below) who swims awkwardly, with fins not streamlined but stocky for holding on—they're prehensile, actually, with an "elbow" joint. What an admirable debut in unabashed yellow on a chalk-white backdrop. This brazen youth is a giant frogfish, who may change color as necessary to gray, brown, black, white, or green. Hawaii ichthyologist John Randall informs that slow-moving, color-blending, benthic (bottom-dwelling) fish have the smallest brain to body ratio of any fish. I, Snorkel Bob,

wonder if these fish laze on a sofa watching TV. Then again, a fish of few words can be a relief, till silence becomes suspect, like a soon-to-be-former spouse, who may mimic the giant frogfish in attempting to eat objects bigger than herself—I mean itself—not like in the courtship phase but with original intent.

The frogfish color change takes a week or 2, but this little guy is clearly in no hurry. So we fast-forward, *et voila . . .*

Photo by Anita

This adult giant frogfish took up residence on a South Maui shallow reef maybe 6–10' deep and stayed for months, holding on against surf and surge and no doubt bulking up in the process. When you ponder a critter who is willing to engorge on prey bigger than itself, you wonder: How does it know how big to go? Maybe it doesn't but simply forges ahead on indomitable spirit. In fact, she kind of looks familiar—Dear, is that you?

Well, I, Snorkel Bob'm joking, of course, perhaps again in poor taste and worse timing, since acrimony and alimony are no laughing matter. I mean really. Still, the arch of the eyebrows and subtle baring of teeth . . . Nah. It couldn't be.

Meanwhile, back on the reef, or close to it at any rate, is an exception to the (general) rule that a young fish should stay close to home. This juvenile dragon wrasse (right) is so named for his dragon-like appendages. As he grows, the appendages shrink; as an adult he's called a rockmover wrasse, because he moves rocks, shoving them aside or turning them over with his snout and forehead, seeking the niblets beneath. Anyway, as a spirited youth, he must be satisfied with rolling pebbles or whatever comes his way, taking shelter in camouflage. He mimics drifting detritus, rolling and tumbling in the current, just like a drifting twig and not like a sweet, juicy little wrasse baby.

The rockmover wrasse here is the same fish as the dragon wrasse on the preceding page. The appendages shrink during maturity, but as an adult, squiggly lines still surround the eyes. This adolescent mug shows the family relation.

On which note we visit a fish who changes even more dramatically from youth to adulthood, the yellowtail coris. The juvenile has no yellow tail and virtually no features of the adult of the species. Neophyte snorkelers in Hawaii easily mistake the juvie yellowtail for a clownfish, what with the bright white patches on the flame-orange body. These juvie yellowtail coris (left and right) enjoy carefree youth.

*Below: A juvie elegant coris (*Kid Elegant?) *in subtle hues that will soon flourish flamboyant.*

Bottom: Not tiny detritus but a brand new baby peacock razor wrasse—a.k.a. a leaf mimic wrasse juvie. Telltale clues are the patterns and single dorsal spike.

Action-oriented and willing to go where few fish have gone, the coris family is a reef favorite. Just for fun, go snake-eyed and scan the inner file for a human counterpart with the same verve, flamboyance and *joie de vivre*. Surely, you'll agree that a mood would be hard-pressed to stay dark, with this mug around.

This tiny 2-spot wrasse froze on camera. Not to worry; he relaxed long enough to vanish in a blink.

Which brings us to our next segment in this subjective study of fishes and who they know and, of more specific gravity, who may know them in return . . .

Above and below: The irrepressible, often tedious but never dull yellowtail coris—the same fish as the juveniles on the previous page, but all grown up. These are males.

Speaking of Mugs

Mug shots, that is, or rather face shots, since these are not the drab, regretful profiles common to the precinct jail but rather the pose suggesting social contact. 2 beings nose to nose are confrontational, possibly threatening. Side by side, they pose no threat. But then friendship often begins on a chance, which may seem risky if you're the 2 oz. nose eyeballing a 200 lb. nose and hoping for friendship. But reef fish are curiously social and willing to take a chance, if the newcomer isn't wearing a gray suit and an overbearing grin, or carrying a net.

Okay, we may as well interrupt this program for a word about . . .

Sharks!

Remember that guy on the right? That's me, Snorkel Bob, back in the day with old Oscar, who's been out of the closet for years now as a trained shark. Oscar's still around, a little longer in the tooth and dining light. It's sardines and crackers mostly, and on occasion some fishcake musubi.

Besides Oscar, we don't see sharks too often in Hawaii, and it's mostly white tip reef sharks when we do. Others here include grays, whale sharks, black tip, Galapagos, el tigre, and a few others. The tigers fascinate most people, with their seemingly innocent movement and nonthreatening appearance. I mentioned this aspect to my friend Darrell, who grew up spearfishing in deep water—the only place spearfishing should occur. He said the easygoing appearance is what makes a tiger dangerous, since they often forego the normal shark behaviors of circling a potential meal a few times with a shrinking radius, or the bodycheck prior to the lunge. A tiger can turn on a heartbeat and take a taste, though sharks in general have excellent vision and keen insight into their menu. They hit what's on it, and don't hit what's not on it. Okay, sometimes they try a taste, and that taste can kill the tastee, but still, they rarely eat what's not on the menu. Besides that, most shark attacks occur in murky water, from shark error, which may be small consolation to the victim, who shouldn't be in murky water. But those victims are often surfers, who have an addiction to breaking waves regardless of murk.

Anyway, Darrell is cool with sharks and only last week was about a mile out from the Makena Resort Hotel in South Maui, looking for ono (wahoo). He admitted that he and his buddy got a couple of decent ono and should have been satisfied, but then they had a bucket of chum left and didn't want to waste it, so they—

"What!" asked I, Snorkel Bob. "Chum?"

Darrell shrugged. He was on the surface when he spied the tiger heading casually for his buddy cruising at depth, about 30'. Darrell's buddy saw the shark and turned to face her at the same moment the shark eyed Darrell on the surface and made a beeline for him, fibrillating stem to stern like they do when they're very excited.

"Wait a minute. This shark wasn't bigger than me, Snorkel Bob, was she?"

Well, yes, about twice as long and 5 times fatter; she was a tiger in the 12' category. Darrell is a fairly humble guy who still suffers a bit of the macho burden—like chumming in deep water and then jumping in to see who might show up.

"Did the sound of your anal sphincter slamming shut scare the shark?"

Darrell hung his head on this note, fessing up that he'd been in the water plenty with tigers, big tigers, too, but had never been charged. It was like a friend had turned on him.

"You chummed!" Yeah, well, what can you do with that action coming on, analyze? No, and Darrell did the only thing he could do, because he is a waterman, and the ocean takes care of its own and vice versa. That is, he didn't want to kill the shark for engaging in its natural behavior, but he was sorely motivated to save his own ass. So he stiff-armed his speargun, and the point hit the shark on the snout. Darrell is bigger than most and strong enough—not to worry, the impact jarred him and the shark, and the shark split.

Don't you love a good shark story? Meanwhile, Darrell said that on closer view, he could see a large fishing hook and a length of steel leader dangling from the shark's lip.

The shark was likely depressed, first a hook in her mouth and then a speargun on her snout as a result of merely seeking some shark snax. Many more tales abound around sharks of all stripes and sizes, but you only hear most on the coconut wireless. That stuff's bad for tourism—okay, 1 more, but I'll keep it short.

It was about '91 when this woman got chomped off Olowalu on Maui. She was said by some to be very nice, socially, but others decried her unfortunate decision to block her section of the beach from local access. She had a friend visiting from Canada, and they were on an a.m. beach stroll when they spied just yonder some splashing and fins, which turned out to be a big tiger or 2 chowing on something dead, which is what they do very well and sometimes get excited about and may even take pride in. At any rate, the unfortunate woman turned to her friend and said, "Oh, come. Let's go swim with the dolphins."

The snorkel biz went to 0 for a few days, followed by 00. The snorkel staff was stumped on correct behavior. By about the 20th call asking me, Snorkel Bob, what they should say, I made it formal: "Tell them it's the ocean, home of many, many sharks. And if they go snorkeling, and a shark doesn't get them, it's really a great feeling."

Well that didn't work either, but again, not to worry. Everything got better by Sunday with a fresh batch of tourii just itching to get in the water. Who knew? Maybe they'd even get lucky enough to swim with the dolphins.

Okay, look again at the top shot on page 40—that yellowtail coris is actually sliding under me, Snorkel Bob, for cover, because look who was cruising over my right shoulder as I was shooting the coris.

Well, it's nice to be noticed, and you know a casual encounter 3" over your shoulder isn't a random contact but a calculated pass to see what's up and if the snax are ready. That's okay; your average white tip reef shark is easy company and socially correct. Here she is again, cruising on out for a profile left.

And close contact with any shark can put a shine on your day, which fairly sums up sharks in Hawaii, except that it doesn't, but I won't go on and on with shark tales to make your skin tighten, except maybe just a bit, beginning with the worst shark horror in Hawaii history: the shark eradication program in the 1970s, when big sharks were caught and killed all over Hawaii. Why? Because the State of Hawaii has a history of mismanaging its reefs. We now know that without apex predators, the reef system will collapse, because the predators just below the sharks will not be in check and will wipe out everything below them.

Okay, here's my last shark story. The title is: "Why We Don't Snorkel in Murky Water."

It was a dark and stormy night—scratch that, it was daytime, blustery with a wind chop. Anita, Gavin, and I, Snorkel Bob, went to Hanauma Bay but found these poor conditions on arrival. Gavin advised swimming through the cut in the ridge between the inside reef and deeper water, then going a quarter mile or so to the right, to a small area known for calm and clarity, Witch's Brew. Against better judgment we went, maintaining inner calm but finding no calm or clear water to the far right. It was more like *Victory at Sea* than *Golden Pond*. So we swam halfway back, maybe 10' apart, when instinct niggled me on the left, where I glanced through murky water to see this phantom outline (right).

He squints for a dorsal fin—but then the shark you see is never so frightening as the one you don't. Was that a fin or a shadow? That one there. He waits for the bump before the hit.
Then he drifts . . .

cf. R. W., *Flame Angels, a novel of Oceania*

No big deal; blacktips are hardly more aggressive than whitetips, and though this muscle-bound cruiser was bigger than me, it wasn't by more than 3 or 4'. My first reaction was to point and shoot, so they'd believe me back on the farm. This shark's casual loll—I could have reached out and touched her—is not aggressive behavior. And I, Snorkel Bob, always feel that a hunky,

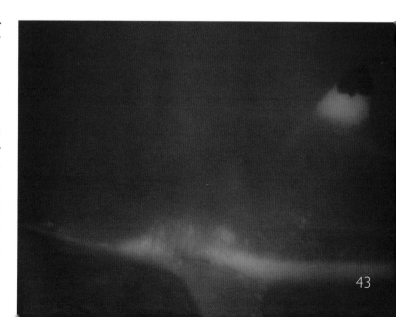

43

muscular shark is far less threatening than a skinny shark. Fat indicates success in the ocean realm, where skinny likely requires an expanded menu to better facilitate odds on survival. Still, this encounter underscores the old rule of snorkeling only in water you can see through.

Yeah, there are plenty more shark tales, like when Snow White got photographed at Molokini a few years ago and then IDed by a Federal Agency that keeps tabs on many sharks from their scars and skin patterns. This great white was a known resident of the Farallon Islands a few miles out from the Golden Gate Bridge. She probably followed a cruise ship to Hawaii. Anyway, the yarns spin on and on, like the baby white tip that showed up at Molokini too, about 18" long, and lived in a cranny, and divers would go by and pull him out by the tail and feed him, which was cute for the first 4' or so. Okay, back to our regularly scheduled programming.

Where was I, Snorkel Bob? Oh, yeah . . .

Frontal mug shots, in which the eyes open on the soul. Some Christian sects claim the absence of souls in nonhuman species. They claim that humans are "known" to have souls, even those humans demonstrating total removal from soulfulness. After all, humans envision God in human form, making human souls a certainty. Yet these Christian clerical humans argue that cats or dogs—or fish—could not possibly have souls. How can heaven allow animals, when your finer restaurants don't?

Well, we could chase this dogma around the block and hump it to death on the corner, but the point should be readily apparent. I, Snorkel Bob, have known a cat and dog and fish or 2 who show more reflection, intuition, compassion, and kindness—and love—than most religious sects seeking conversion of untrammeled regions to better export resources. Most humans experience instant friendship at some point in life, and some humans experience it on a reef. Some find fast friends on a regular basis in nonhuman society. So?

So if we can view this contact as ordinary rather than extraordinary, we may proceed to social order, community, values, material needs, and so on.

No matter how shy a fish may be at first encounter, nearly every fish—or sea creature—will warm to social contact with time and especially with repeated visits. This isn't rocket or marine science or a cosmic revelation; it's merely true, proven by the tenets of Column 3. Can a friendship emerge? Of course, by the simple law of familiarity. Some species are innately less inclined to camaraderie, like, say, sea snakes, anemones, and most crustaceans, who may well fear the dreaded lemon/butter sauce.

Oh, and flounders. Note the minimal warmth and fuzz with no loss of social grace. Some fish blend with the landscape to avoid mundane gladhanding, chitchat on weather, current trends, or predatory behavior. Color and texture makes these beauties stand out, though these fish do seem more aloof than some.

Even creatures at the top of the intelligence totem, like octopuses and squibs—I mean squids—may seem like cold fish, but they're not. I mean they are, literally, just as you are so many grams of nitrogen, potassium, and phosphorous. Socially speaking, we're all more, if we recognize the God-given characteristics of any living creature, some of whom eat other creatures and kill to do so. We need not belabor the species that kills more than all others combined; suffice to say that marine invertebrates tend to be reserved . . .

I first called this octopus shot "Not a Baboon's Ass," but a glib moment can lose a lasting, lyrical value, in this case an unforgettable communion with a circumspect but open-minded octopus living off that same beach park on Moorea in French Polynesia, between Opanohu and Cook's Bays. Okay, so what do I, Snorkel Bob, call it now? How about: "Highbrow Encounter"? Or maybe: "The Morning After"? No, no—there I go again. It'll come to me.

Meanwhile, the next shot (below) is from the island of Huahine, also in the Society Islands chain of French Polynesia. You won't see antler coral like this in Hawaii, because of human traffic everywhere. You won't see it in French Poly either, in water less than 5' deep, because the humans can't help destroying what they can reach—in this case they stand on it, as a matter of convenience or maybe a lack of conciousness.

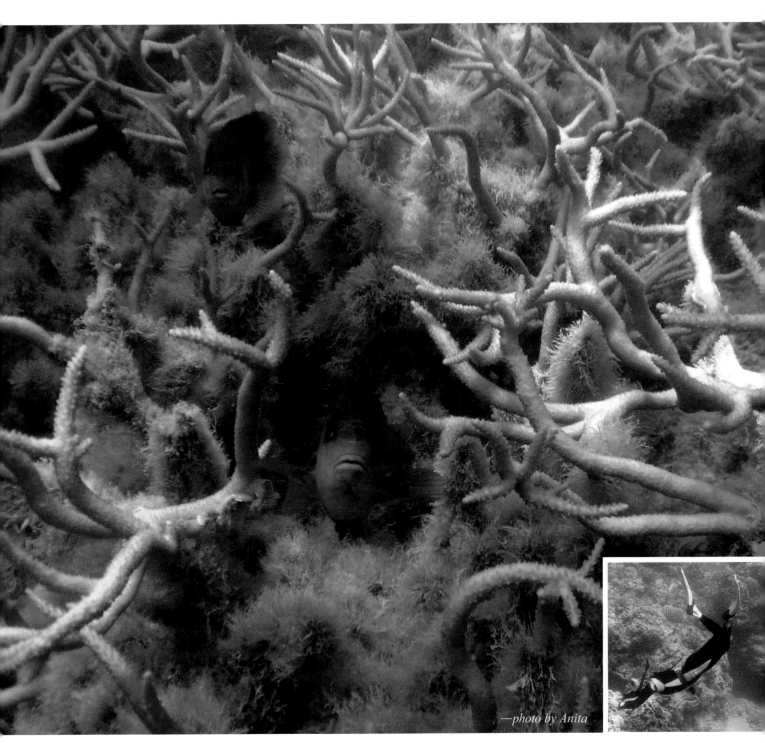

—photo by Anita

"Not Dressed Up for Halloween in an Elk Costume"?

This Hawaii kama'aina *(left top and middle)* is a Pacific Gregory, lovable for his skittish, uncertain defense of something behind him. He'll toe the line—or fin the line, at any rate—showing the bravado of a reef-smart fish who knows his way around. From the side, his intermittent gray-brown and dark-flecked scales look irregular, but they're not. He'll scram in a heartbeat if you keep coming on, but not before a nice family portrait.

Lower left is a blue-eyed damsel, and she is demure, coy, and hard to get as a fish coquette ever was.

To the right, a big-scale soldierfish.

Parlez-vous humma humma?

48

Uh, do you owe me any money?

The juvenile (1") multiband butterflyfish (left) couldn't resist checking out the arms, cords, lens, and port, and maybe he wanted to show his natural grace in a sudden pirouette and greeting.

Baby Huey (right) just wanted to say "hey."

And some fish are gregarious, gadabout, in your face, as it were. This blueline butterflyfish (above) is socially confident. This species is so severely depressed on some Hawaii reefs that the Department of Land and Natural Resources says it is "experiencing a 100% decline."

In honest English, "It's gone."

Helloo.

This convict tang (manini, left) is simply curious—and unafraid.

The front and center stance can be a line in the sand, but that's probably not the case with this extroversive yellowtail coris (below). My, Snorkel Bob's, best guess is that he's taking advantage of his reflection in the lens to practice saying "humuhumunukunukuapua'a."

Left, an engaging humuhumulei, *or lei triggerfish.*

The Hawaiian whitespotted toby (this page) generally appears to be content, and often has a companion nearby for regular visual and physical contact. The baby face and even disposition seems a mix of curiosity and tolerance, while their puffy bellies can be a mix of recent meal, young'uns, and parasitic worms.

Snorkel Bob! Must you?

You were there. I know you were there. Don't deny it. Fish saw you there.

Hawaiian spotted puffers (above) aren't exactly joyful in humanoid company but will mug for the camera, while a crown toby (below) is more skittish.

This juvenile Hawaiian spotted boxfish (below) is female, and may morph to male (above) if the current dominant male goes south.

Portrait of the artist as a young Hawaiian spotted boxfish.

You know it's hard out there for a fish.

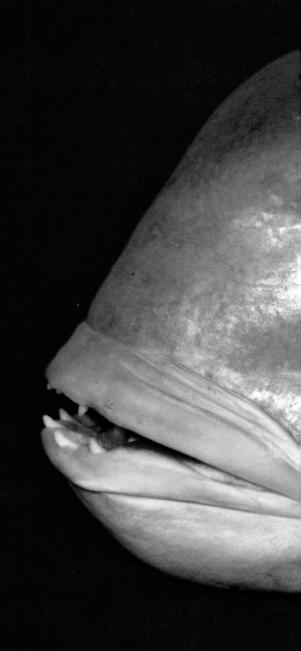

Well, hello, little fish. What's your name?

Peacock Razorfish

The Profiles

n which a gillbreather reveals the joys and sorrows of being a fish. The bluefin trevally (left) went 80–90 lb. and swam in circles, likely over a hiding place where a trembling snack was taking cover. She didn't defend the spot aggressively but rather tolerated company, patiently awaiting the surrender of her next meal. Jacks often team with other species—commonly with moray eels—in hunting forays, where one covers the hidden exit as the other rushes the front door. Payouts are generally balanced. This bruiser doesn't pussyfoot around but jams the jambs too—note the facial scarring, worse than Al Pacino as a psychotic drug lord—likely from jamming rocky crevasses to get at whomever cowers inside.

Butterflyfish are far more oppressed than most other species, because of massive extraction by the aquarium trade. Many Hawaii reefs are now butterflyfish-free zones resulting from unregulated take. The Hawaii Department of Land and Natural Resources calls this "fishery management," seeking maximum catch revenue. These fish wholesale out of Hawaii to the aquarium trade at $3–4 on average. They retail on the mainland and across Europe and Asia for 10 times that amount, leaving chump change in Hawaii, which, historically is for chumps. I, Snorkel Bob, will not begin another rant here, except to recall our late, great President of the United States of America, who looked east, eye to eye with the Red Menace, and said it best: "Mr. Gorbachev, tear *down* this aquarium!"

The aquarium catchers generally raid a reef community with a wholesale order in hand that needs to be filled. Not finding the target fish ordered, the catchers will take what's in reach, making them far less than a "fishery." I, Snorkel Bob, hate casting shadows on this celebration of interspecies communion, but this situation appears to be—let's see, what's the word? Oh, yeah, immoral. Is someone throwing a Sunday punch at Mother Nature, or is it just me being unreasonable? Do you know what my Uncle Mikhail finally had to do?

Never mind. Butterflyfish naturally occur everywhere—over 2 dozen species should be able to thrive in abundance on Hawaii reefs, way beyond "sustainable" (Bah!) levels. Yet their populations are down, even in

protected areas. For example, the blueline butterflyfish (right) is found nowhere in the world but Hawaii, where it was commonly seen until recently. Now the species is very rare. Is it endangered? Species protection in the United States is generally available through 1) a Convention on International Trade in Endangered Species of Wild Fauna and Flora (CITES) listing, 2) the Lacey Act, regulating wildlife transport AND recognizing state and local government authority to protect local species, AND the best known protection: 3) the Endangered Species Act. But listing requires a species census, a hugely expensive challenge on terra firma and far more costly underwater. A fish census can take years and more money than will ever be available. The Kona State Division of Aquatic Resources

(DAR) completed a fish count recently on 2 key reefs. At Puako on the North Kona Coast, blueline butterflies are down 98%, while at Honaunau farther south (City of Refuge) they're gone—*finito, caput, no mo stay*, or as DAR put it, *"experiencing a 100% decline."*

The aquarium industry denies responsibility with loud accusation at other causes, claiming a continuing right to empty reefs—to remove these fish for sale to an amusement industry in a faraway place.

Also devastated on these 2 telltale reefs is the teardrop butterflyfish (left). "Sustainable" often means minimal; i.e., by leaving a few brood pairs, humanity "allows" a species to survive far below levels intended by nature. The alternative approach to sustainable is an abundance of fish: what the Hawaiian archipelago had for aeons, up to 50 years ago. Humanity has a regrettable pattern in recent centuries of obliterating other species. The consequences today are far greater.

Among the abundantly supportable butterflyfishes is the threadfin butterfly (lower left), with a threadlike trailer on its dorsal fin. The raccoon butterfly (above and below) has a raccoon mask and a propensity to school, like this.

The pyramid butterfly (above) has a pyramid on its flank and is notable for gathering in dramatic vertical columns on the back wall of Molokini Crater near Maui and elsewhere.

The forceps butterfly (right) is named for its long snout. Am I, Snorkel Bob, greedy or motivated by self-interest for wanting to see these fish by the hundreds?
Just call me Snorkel Scrooge.

A milletseed butterfly (above) in reflective repose.

The whitespotted surgeonfish (right) is obviously named for its obstreperous white spots, like this beauty in Manele Bay on Lanai.

71

The ornate butterfly, a huge favorite, is heavily taken by the aquarium trade—and often shipped with a live guarantee ranging from 0 to 15 days. Unfortunately the ornate butterflyfish survives only on a diet of live coral, without which it will starve (to death) in

30 days. Sorry for the discouraging words, but without shedding light on something wrong, a solution will rarely emerge.

Among the 17 damselfish species seen in Hawaii are a few chromis. A whimsical and sometimes plentiful chromis is the chocolate-dip, named for the arduous and loving process by which Neptune holds each fish by the tail at birth for a dip into the chocolate. Though skittish and easily spooked back into cover, these little beauties show exquisite detail in design and color.

This brings us to that stalwart defender of color and style, the parrotfish, or *uhu*. The parrot is obviously named for its beak, with a few individuals in dazzling turquoise over amber and lavender. The parrot also suffers from indiscriminate, unregulated (no limits) extraction from Hawaii reefs. The carnage is made more egregious by taking place at night when scuba divers with spearguns can drop onto a reef and pluck the sleeping parrots like berries from a vine.

But they are hardly as resilient as berries; the parrotfish, or *uhu,* population is down. To this day, the State of Hawaii has yet to regulate spearfishing on compressed or surface-supplied air, or at night. Often noted as the lynchpin species of any reef, *uhu* allow reefs to survive by controlling algae and making sand. The coral shown here was likely grazed by a parrotfish.

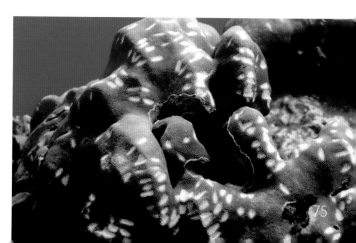

On a curious note, uhu *are hermaphroditic. The Pacific bullethead parrotfish shown here (below) begin life as either male or female, and then, as far as I, Snorkel Bob, can tell, some change color and/or gender, while some change only one and not the other, while others change both, like humans, kind of. On a happy note, this fish is the inspirational icon of the South Maui Uhu SC (scooter club) renowned for frequent circumnavigations and even more frequent snorkel stops along the way.*

The peacock razorfish (facing page, bottom right) is always colorful and always engaging. This young'un, at home near an eel garden, would not allow passage without a screen test. These engaging beauties drift like flotsam as juveniles. All dive into the sand at the first blink of danger. Some fish watchers theorize that the shape here mimics a drifting leaf, with the erect dorsal spine meant to look like a stem. The color appears to blend with the substrate.

Wrasses and parrots are both hermaphrodites with confusing color changes, but they are 2 different families.

You talkin' to me?

Hey, I gotta go! (blackside razorfish, adult, diving into sand).

Among the most colorful reef species are the angelfish. I'll be brief on the downside: The aquarium collectors hammer the angels, no limits. With luck, diligence, and growing support, this too will change.

On the brighter side, angelfish encounters can brighten an otherwise average day. Hardly gregarious, or for that matter even social, most angels are skittish and shy and take cover quickly. The flame angel, hunted to invisibility in Hawaii, is perhaps the shyest of all.

These flame angels are also on a Tahiti reef. Few humans have seen one in Hawaii, and fewer still have seen 2. I, Snorkel Bob, have seen 2 in Hawaii, but it took several decades and I dasn't say where. You may note that *Flame Angels* is also a novel of Oceania, dealing with the joys and sorrows most near to my heart.

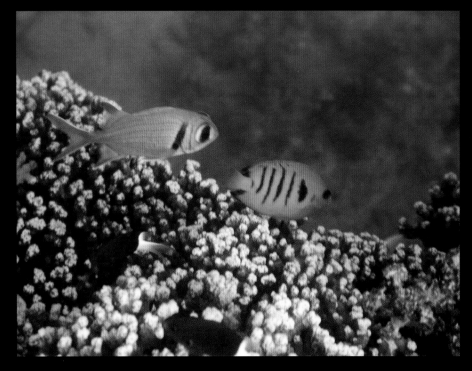

Another dazzling introvert of French Polynesia is the lemonpeel angel (right), with its irrepressible yellow and brilliant blue eyeliner. They tease and taunt with seductive poses and flashing flamboyance, but the lemonpeel angel remains elusive.

Potter's angelfish are another favorite who will pose for ½ a heartbeat before darting to cover. All the angelfishes are skittish, quick and shy. They dart for cover into coral that looks impenetrable. I, Snorkel Bob, got shots of hundreds of Potter's angels that weren't so bad, till stumbling across this little honey (2 pages down) who couldn't get enough of showbiz. I suspect intrigue with the reflection in the lens port, or maybe it was a tawdry flirtation. Either way, it's a satisfied shutterbug who gets clarity on a reef gem like this one.

Hardly as quick as a Potter's angel, this timorous pup could well be a giant porcupinefish who immigrated south to Tahiti, fleeing the aquarium scourge. The Hawaii State Senate's Water and Land Committee hearing in 2008 heard an aquarium collector testify that he must empty reefs, because he has 4 kids to feed and payments on his boat, engine, and trailer. Then there's the fuel and insurance and another kid on the way, which means a 2nd washing machine and dryer to handle diapers, because the disposable diapers are just too expensive for a working man. Besides that, "Why shouldn't we take puffers? We see them on almost every reef, so why shouldn't we take them? You have no data that says we shouldn't take them."

So this puffer went south to Tahiti. Wouldn't you?

That's a tough mug to follow, what with the peekaboo to see if the coast is clear. I, Snorkel Bob, would be stumped to match it, but as usual, I think I can—with a mug of what's watching me right now, like she has been for 19 years. Well, not 19 for another 4 months, but still, it's way past 18½.

Flojo at 18.

Hey, you schlep a camera and lights and a passel o' crap all over the place and then risk life 'n limb getting a bunch o' frikkin fish shots, not to mention insult to injury with a lowbrow bunch trying to strip-mine the reefs, and then you got the foul weather and sharks and worse yet, floaters, because the State of Hawaii won't outlaw charter boat dumping (I shitchu not), and then the software expense and the financial risk of putting a book together during a Depression and trying for Oprah and having some no-neck schlump ask what the F in Snorkel F. Bob stands for . . .

Then YOU can run a picture of YOUR cat! Okay?

Meanwhile, I got some eel shots. Okay?

photo by *Fernando*

Garden Party

"I went to a garden party, to reminisce with my old friends . . ."

Hey, Ricky Nelson never had it this good. He had to put up with a bunch of snooty rockers who didn't want him to be the new Ricky Nelson but insisted that he stay the same.

It's not like that on a reef—or a sandy patch of bottom—where adaptability is your primary alternative to perishability. Just look at these rockers swing . . .

Garden eels are every marine photographer's challenge. Actually only about 2' long and skinny as a cheroot, they seem bigger than they are. Most notable, however, is their eerily swaying choreography that ends abruptly as the whole chorus line vanishes in a blink—into cover, if an obtrusive intruder approaches too quickly. The eels at Molokini Crater off Maui maintain a stable community at about 55', and though they suffer endless tourist traffic, they've become familiar, too, so it seems like they're a tad more approachable. I, Snorkel Bob, planned a slow approach, inching nearer on my elbows for a better shot. I got advised that the elbow walk is a bad idea, because these eels feel the elbow vibration through the sand. "Pshaw," said I, Snorkel Bob, or rather a more seasoned expletive to that effect, and on in I elbowed, inch by inch, *et voila!*

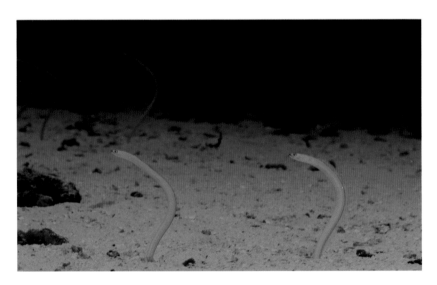

I call this one "Fred and Ginger." Get it?

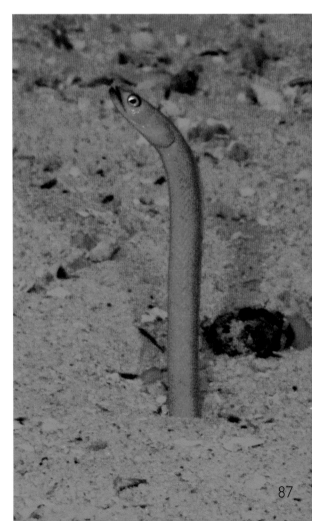

And this solo shot fairly captures the emotional range of your average garden eel.

Most surprising is the peripheral community hovering near the eels—razor wrasses and yellowfin surgeonfish, mostly, with a lugubrious sea cucumber slogging along behind. Or maybe he's just meditating.

Next are the moray eels.

They're so cute at that age—hardly a foot long and ready to eat off your hand, right up the to the elbow*. Not really. That's a joke, poorly timed and ill advised yet again, which may be a chronic condition for me, Snorkel Bob. *cf. Popeye the sailor man

This toothy fellow (below) scared the snot outa me, Snorkel Bob, as I pursued a pesky Potter's who wouldn't hold still, so we rounded to the crest of a coral mound to find Big Boy waiting. He turned casually my way and nearly said "Aaahhhloha."

This baby yellow margin moray (above) is about as big as your pinky. Peeking out of her tiny hole, she appears happy on Maui's north shore.

Her very big brother (right) is huge in stature and tooth. This big yellow margin moray seemed casually receptive to visitors.

Kukla, the yellow margin moray.

Eels look ferocious in most profiles, especially when waking up from nappy poo with a big yawn, exposing rows of inverse choppers—including a row or 2 along the roof of the mouth for a SURE GRIP while tearing flesh. Most often, they're only pumping water over their gills. A big eel named Garbanzo used to live at Reef's End, Molokini. Garbanzo worked for the dive companies, whose macho leaders loved to show bravado by feeding Garbanzo dead squibs—I mean squids—from a plastic bag. One day a one-up wingnut removed his regulator and put the squid in his mouth, so that Garbanzo could give him a kiss on taking the squid.

All eels are myopic and far more dependent on scent than vision; Garbanzo could not see the squid at its usual range but knew it was out there, so he made his move, mouth open, snagging the squib—I mean squid—and snagging the macho idiot's—I mean the dive leader's—jugular vein on the way past.

The story ended with blue-green blood gushing from the "leader's" neck in a perfect illustration of all color going to blue and green below 40'. This was 65'. Anyway, for some reason unknown, nobody died, though the bad rap went to Garbanzo, who left town soon after.

THE TRUTH is, some eels are aggressive and will bite a diver's hand as he reaches into a hole for a lobster or octopus (what a tough break for the diver). HOWEVER, most eels are cold, cuddly creatures with no more snap than my dog Lulu, who might hurt a flea (if she had one, which she doesn't), but otherwise wants nothing more than to share the love and dog biscuits that make the world go round.

Lulu the Wonderdog (right), doing her now-famous giant moray eel impersonation.

Which brings us to . . .

Multiband Butterflyfish in tandem, a cold and fuzzy romance on the reef.

Reef Love

Because of an abundance of color, affection, grace, and the most exquisite balance nature has to offer, the reef is a place of bonding, for fishy romance, symbiosis, or a random schmooze.

Random schmooze? Snorkel Bob, you've taken this whimsy over the top. Fish don't schmooze, random or otherwise. Do they?

Well, yes, they do. Company is where you find it, like here in the water column, as if meeting by chance in outer space.

These 2 Hawaiian dascyllus may be a mated pair, indicated by body language in synchronous choreography. In this case, one veered up and the other down to better see the imposing but apparently harmless creature approaching. Damselfish often stay near a home coral head that they defend with aggressive movement toward anyone approaching, but these 2 may be out for a cruise, to see where else the damsel 2-step might take them.

This Potter's angel and goldring surgeon seem to know or recognize or sense each other in the flow of reef contact, where society among varying species has a unique order, and so does the community at large.

And speaking of large . . .

. . . the Hawaiian cleaner wrasse may provide the biggest show on the reef. Scientists often profile a reef species as charismatic—or not, and few fish or people can outshine the Hawaiian cleaner wrasse. Apparently happy and usually busy, this fish goes where few fish dare to go. When a cleaner wrasse or 2 set up a cleaning station, other fish will literally wait in line for a grooming. Many fish spread their dorsal spines or gill covers—or jaws—so the cleaner can get in there all the better to pluck the goobers and parasites.

Every fish needs a grooming, even a sleek unicornfish who would intimidate most others in the snax-size category.

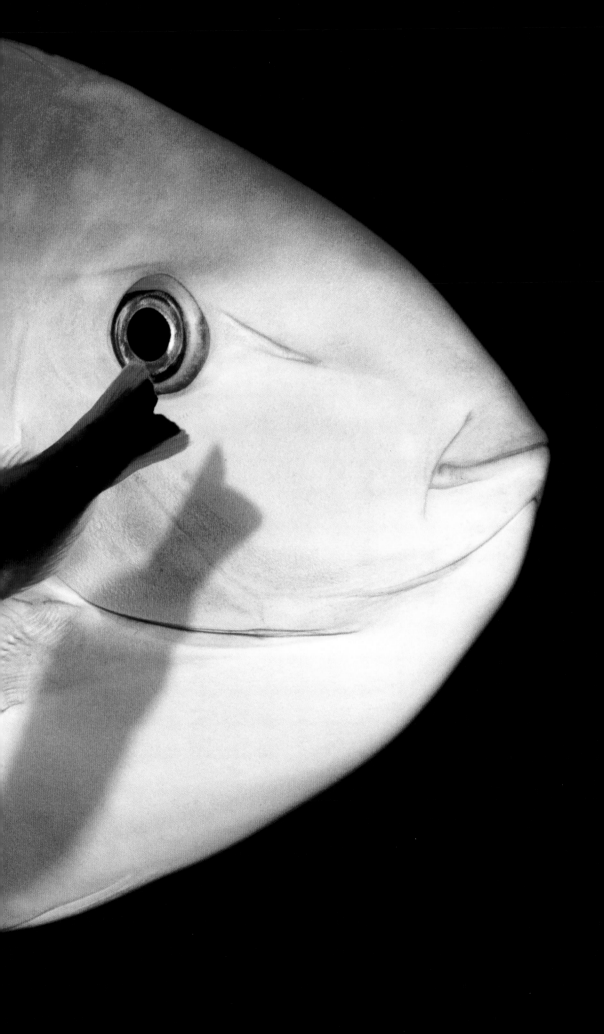

Hey, turn around.

Now hold still.

Okay, you're spotless.

Hey, have you been brushing and flossing?

Next.

Some friendships are hard to avoid.

Cornet cruising as viewed through the port of Apollo XIX.

2 goats in a crowd.

Moorish idols, a species unto themselves, often cruise in pairs.

Once upon a time there was a fisherman whose wife was never satisfied . . . Yes, these indigo dartfish are the same as the famed fish granting 3 wishes.

These bluestreak gobies (above) stayed close to home, in Tahiti, likely guarding a brood nest . . .

. . . while this goldsaddle goatfish couple roamed an acre of reef nonstop at medium high speed, in tandem.

Coachmen (left) or pennant bannerfish often school on Tahiti reefs to pluck snax therefrom. The high aspect ratio dorsal and anal fins make them efficient swimmers and graceful in a current.

The 4some below are a young psychedelic wrasse, goldring surgeon, elegant coris, and whodaguy jostling for cover, or maybe to see if I, Snorkel Bob, might want to school up and, you know, cruise.

Bottom: George and Gracie are achilles tangs—herbivores, keeping algae in check.

These 2 gilded triggerfish at Molokini Crater pressed gill plates for a curlicue dance in the water column. It looked like a mating ritual, except that these (right) are both bull triggers and not likely demonstrating alternate sexual preference. So the communion here may be a mysterious dominance play to claim a prize, either territory or some prime triggerfish puhe—or both! How thoroughly, naturally macho. Don't you think?

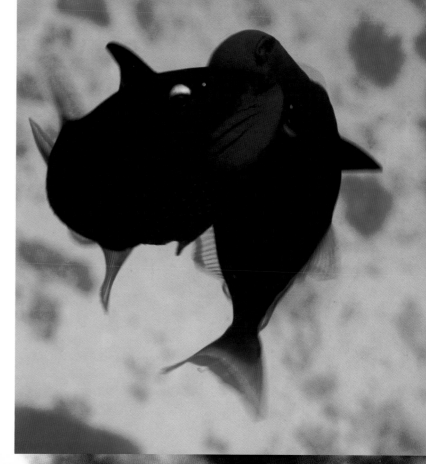

And this fair beauty (below) is the she-trigger. NOTE the coy flirtation. Look familiar?

Octodogging—actually,
he carries the message in his
fingertips.
Who knew?

Could we have some
privacy here?

Octo postcoital.

Defender, voyeur, or misguided competitor? None of the above; this shameless doublebar goat (below) is hovering for stray chum. Oh, it gets down, gets funky, gets loose on the reef, often less constrained than 42nd St., but purer, cleaner, and closer my love to thee.

Schooling

Schooling goatfish, or weke *(veh-keh), on South Maui, with a gathering of the herbivore clans nearby.*

Convict tangs (above), Hawaii and Indo Pacific sargeants (lower right), and a chromis school (below) cavort on a pinnacle, catching sunbeams.

A needlefish school swims with sunbeams in the shallows of Kona Harbor (below).

Akule *this thick (above) draw netters, which draw tigers; best to snorkel the other way.*

Below is a Hawaiian dascyllus (domino damselfish) jammie party with a pink durgon chaperone.

Sea Turtles

you shall have.

The Hawaiian green sea turtle, or *honu*, prevails in Hawaii waters, back from the brink and more—conditioned to familiarity with humans, a trust for the new reef order. Here is a healthy *honu*, close up.

Another turtle girl had her heart set on me, Snorkel Bob.

I don't worry about the men in gray suits (sharks), but do keep a 3rd eye open to peripheral movement in the jumbo category. Apex predators are mostly figmental, but seeing a turtle or 2 is comforting; who better to indicate all clear? Who could sneak up on a seasoned snorkel exec anyway? So I'm cruising medium shallow, focusing on a green-eyed batfish, when suddenly below—in kissing distance—is a *honu* around 350 lb., coming under for the mount up, as it were. I'm not attracted to turtles in that way, but the offer was compelling; think of the offspring. Such zeal, wit, color, flourish, candor—and what flippers! Ah, well, our sweet time together was brief, parting most likely for the best.

Hey, Sailor. Buy a turtle a drink?

Ah, to think, to wish, to dream what might have been.

This honu *in Ahihi Bay on South Maui enjoys a shell grooming by her symbiotic pals, goldring surgeons. It's a soothing grooming for one with the tasty shell goobers for the others.*

Afflicting *honu* for a few years now has been the fibropapilloma virus, manifesting in white tumors that eventually kill the turtle. They usually appear near the eyes and shoulders. FP is an immunity disorder believed to stem from dirty oceans worldwide. A good book on this and ocean conditions in general is *Fire in the Turtle House* by Osha Gray Davidson.

This honu *(right) shows a small FP tumor on her eye: a bad sign, though remission is possible.*

This honu *is severely ill, so blind it would have plowed right through me. FP appears to be on the decline. This* extra large honu *may intimidate predators with its size, but will surely succumb soon.*

But wait! We interrupt this program for these shots by Anita, main mermaid to me, Snorkel Bob, and personal friend of a *honu* or 2, as well as a few *honu 'ea*. *Honu* means Hawaiian green sea turtle, and *honu 'ea* means hawksbill turtle. *'Ea* is Hawaiian for red—hawksbills were hunted to near-extinction for their reddish shells. They weren't eaten, because they feed on sponges that carry the ciguatera virus present in many reef fish. Cumulative up the food chain and harmless to those fish, ciguatera is not so indifferent to humans, who itch for 2 years and then die, a tough break indeed. Hawksbills are still critically endangered in Hawaii.

NOTE: *Hawksbill Babies at Oneloa, the Movie*, is 21 minutes of hawksbills hatching and making for the surf and is still free to educators around the world at www.snorkelbob.com—you pay the freight.

But enough falderal. Ladies and gentlemen, boys and girls, I give you . . .

Honuanita

and a few pics from her family album, beginning with . . .

This hawksbill mama is Orion, the star of the show on South Maui, good for 5 or 6 nests every 3 or 4 years. Rigged with satellite telemetry and a proven survivor of the odds and elements, Orion is well known and loved. This is first light at Oneloa (meaning long sands, a.k.a. Makena Beach) as Orion plods seaward after depositing her clutch of 150–200 eggs.

Can you imagine the excitement 60 days later, mas o menos, *when:*

This femme turtale *(above and below) is a regular habitue on a favorite S. Maui reef. The wee turtlets to the right are tasting freedom after 60 days, more or less, incubating under the sand.*

Surf's up.

On the preceding page are hawksbill turtles, *honu 'ea*.
On these pages are Hawaiian green sea turtles, *honu*.

This honu *will likely survive, in time sloughing the hook in its mouth—and so would you.*

Okay, I can't take it anymore. It's . . .

Yellow Tang Time

Yellow tangs are surgeonfish, herbivores who work all day keeping reefs healthy by preventing algae buildup. They also leave Hawaii reefs by the thousands every day, shipped to the mainland United States, Europe, and Asia for a brief life in the aquarium trade. Estimates on aquarium extraction in Hawaii range from a reported official catch of 2 million fish per year to estimates by State scientists of up to 10 million fish per year. The aquarium collectors have no limits on their catch and no limits on the number of catchers. They have no limits on rare, charismatic, or endemic species, or on species known to die quickly in captivity. Hawaiian cleaner wrasses die quickly without many other fish to clean. Ornate butterflyfish and other butterflies starve (to death) in 30 days without live coral to graze, but they ship out daily with a 15-day live guarantee.

The aquarium trade is not "sustainable" or morally acceptable. The aquarium trade has branded me, Snorkel Bob, as a a reef hugger and emotional zealot, and I concede—though I think they're mostly upset by my analogy comparing them to the guys on MSNBC who get lured onto some fresh teenager bait, only to find that it's a sting, with national cameras rolling. Wait a minute—am I saying that these guys are actually defiling reefs with the same wicked secrecy as those nasty guys on TV?

Well, what else can you say? The most ardent, outspoken, and aggressive defender of the aquarium trade in Hawaii is the State Division of Aquatic Resources in Kona, hub of Hawaii's aquarium industry. The State manages this crime as a "fishery," for optimal extraction and monetary return—a pattern of the past. Maximum resource extraction was 1st introduced by the missionaries.

All parties agree on one thing: the total annual catch—whether it's a few million "ornamental" fish or a few million more "ornamental" fish—is 60% yellow tangs. They live up to 40 years on the reef, but 99% of all yellow tangs sold into aquarium slavery die within a year, many in transit.

We used to see them by the thousands in Hawaii. Many reefs are now void. Along with a few humble reef huggers crying out in Hawaii, another tremulous voice resounds through history. It was our own beloved President of the United States of America, Ronald Reagan, who demanded, "Mr. Gorbachev! Tear *down* this aquarium!"

On a brighter note, you can still see yellow tangs and others in semi-abundance at a few protected areas on Maui and in Kona.

The United States tang-erines (below) take porkchop coral head (reenactment), while a young recruit (left) looks on in admiration.

It's tang time. The money shot on a yellow tang is with full dorsal fin extension (left), indicating (to me, Snorkel Bob) relaxed engagement. Dorsal folded back appears to be the fright and flight posture. The catch is, juvenile yellow tangs (below) always have their dorsal fins fully unfurled and their ribs visible. Who knows? Maybe it's a defensive posture meant to mimic something more formidable on the visual plane.

Hey, Paul, wait for me!

Hey, wait a minute . . . Whodaguy?

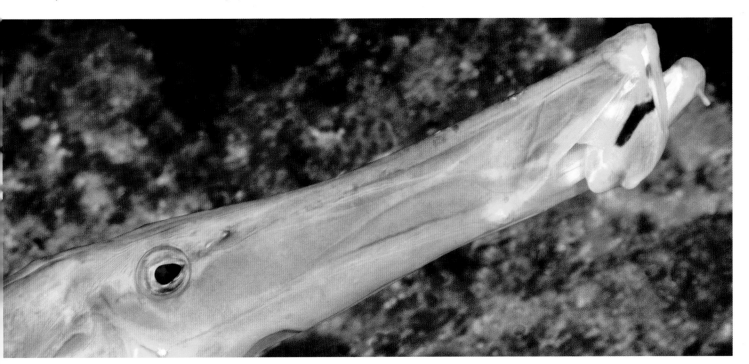

    It's a trumpetfish in yellow tang clothing—the same individual you saw mere minutes ago in mottled gray green. Trumpets change color to blend in, for offense rather than defense, to better ask the small fry if they might like some candy, or perhaps a nice ride in a Cadillac. This might be devious but factors adaptive skills some predators must use to earn a living. At the top, or apex, on the other hand, predatory behavior is far simpler . . .

Ulua Akea, *Giant Trevally*

Ulua
the big jacks

These lunkers in the 80–90 lb. range take no guff, but they're also oddly engaging, curious, social, and willing to cruise or hunt in symbiosis.

Do you have some Neosporin?

Ulua Bluefin Trevally

Sometimes emotive, bluefin trevally (above and upper left) commonly show blue dots on shimmering greenish skin with a gold luster.

Great ulua (lower left) are not so much colorless as well matched to their surroundings. Ulua are easygoing and may be the big bass drum behind the tiny chimes.

The reef shrimp above are rare in Hawaii now. The banded reef shrimp below lives in Tahiti; he may have fled to avoid oppressive conditions in Hawaii, where reefs are voided of critical species with no management, no regulation, and no protection, in deference to an amusement industry in a faraway land—i.e., the aquarium trade in the United States, Europe, and Asia.

Many species once abundant in Hawaii are gone. Many reef shrimp species were plentiful in Hawaii not so long ago. Now they thrive far south, in . . .

Tahiti

So we reach a moment of delicate balance, with disconsolate grief on the one hand, while on the other is a new world to embrace. Oceania comes on in waves. A dewy, green tint clearly casts the heat-rippled haze in the past and the future, converged at last in a continual moment; regret and hope, longing and fulfillment are now. This balance is both cause and antidote for doubt. No sooner does a forlorn man hark back than he's thrust ahead, to a dream of what might be. And here it is, moist and dilated, receptive as a tropical maiden unhindered by missionary tabu ever could be.

Strolling forward, innocent and blissful into a happily ever after, the wide-eyed child of misfortune and the seasoned man of the world become one. Tropical beauty with very few human people is only vaguely recalled in Hawaii. Opening his arms in acceptance, he feels the vibration—still a man off kilter, listing to port, unhinged and not quite connected, he makes the turn into the home stretch, very near to feeding the hunger and quenching the thirst. The monkish might call this an illusion, a deception of the life process, whereby desire seeks fulfillment, yet their itchy garments, celibacy, silence, saltines and water might comprise a lust of a different nature, a perversion unique to their strange appetite and quest. But let no appetite or quest be dismissed, if the pilgrim harms no other in seeking sustenance and meaning.

I, waterman, am here.

—from *Flame Angels, a novel of Oceania*

Similar to the Hawaiian lionfish is this spotfin lionfish, still abundant down south but gone to aquarium captivity in Hawaii. Pennant bannerfish (left) are extremely shy. This beauty lives in Taaroa, on the island of Tahiti.

139

Tahiti cornets (above) are very similar to Hawaii cornets.

Blueline damsel (left).

The chromis (right) show up blue, turquoise, and emerald, often on the same coral head, but become virtually invisible in the water column.

The damselfish (right) is similar to Hawaii damsels in shape and behavior, with variant color patterns. Note that Tahiti damsels often use big anemones as habitat, just like clown anemonefish.

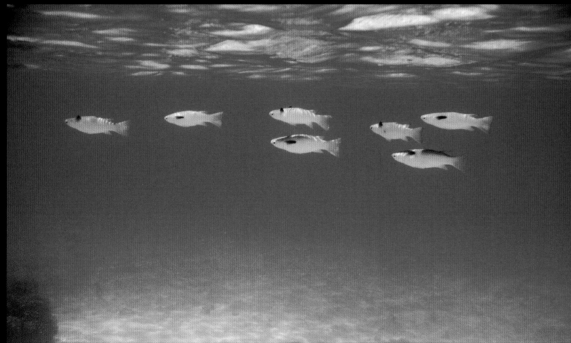

Who would travel so far to see a handful of mullet at sunset?

The Indian toby (right) is easy on the eyes, with its gentle curiosity and incandescent color pattern.

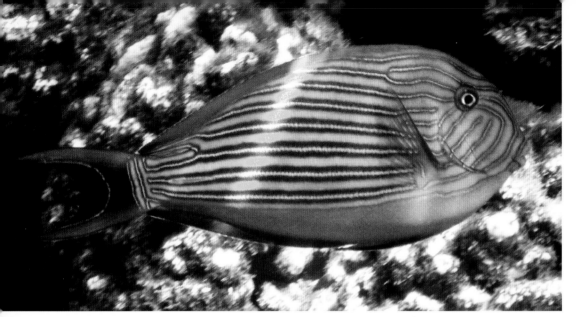

The striped surgeonfish (left) and the regal angelfish (middle) are 2 of hundreds of Oceania species comprising an alternate reality in the shallows.

The playful pup below is a stonefish in the Society Islands of French Polynesia, under a sidewalk fronting a small boat anchorage on the island of Huahine.

Among the most venomous fish in the oceans, the stonefish dorsal spine can inject a quick cure to your woes.

Au revoir, pour maintenant, mes enfants . . .

Now can you see the stonefish?

Just a few of

Your Wrasses

including diverse types such as the coris, with special mention of the parrotfish, which is not a wrasse but effuses similiar color and joy . . .

*R*eef and Shore Fishes of the *Hawaiian Islands* by renowned ichthyologist John Randall is a treasure trove of detail on Hawaii fishes. Randall counts 453 total wrasse species, with 45 species in Hawaii, and discoveries continuing. They range from 2" to 5½'—the giant humphead wrasse. To me, Snorkel Bob, of the See and Ye Shall Know school, wrasses share 4 distinct characteristics: 1) colors and patterns that are often flamboyant, and may change with gender and age; 2) a short, darting motion with a subtle up and down, as if sinking slightly at the end of a stroke and rising again on each fin propulsion. The wrasse stroke is singular—they swim with their pectoral fins; 3) all wrasses are carnivorous (fish, plankton, parasites); and 4) many have a cigar shape and a willing social engagement often surpassing the boundaries of good taste; wrasses can be extroversive, in your

face as well as those of other fishes. Aggressive wrasses can indicate tourists with fish food in the area—those who love the reef do not feed the fish. Fish food makes them fat as well as constipated and keeps them from their natural duties.

Ornate wrasses (left and above) looking blushingly ornate.

Pink pencil wrasses, starring in La Vie en Rose!

This Christmas wrasse may look confused, since Congress took up the issue and may soon change its name to holiday wrasse. Not really, though I, Snorkel Bob, regret the absence of a Hanukkah wrasse and may well appropriate this one.

*Often animated,
the saddle wrasses
stand out for playful
attitude and a cartoon
appearance.*

Eightline wrasse.

These bird
wrasses are
named for their
protuberance. Right
is a female and far
right is a male.

Both fish here are smalltail wrasse adults. The blue-green one in the inset is a male, commonly called a pencil wrasse.

*And this Ruby, Ruby, Ruby beauty is a female,
but surely you could tell.*

The off chance of a few

Random Encounters

The fang blenny doesn't look like a Hawaiian cleaner wrasse, but it mimics a cleaner's attitude, stance, and positioning, inviting other fish and an unsuspecting snorkeler or diver to line up for a scale grooming. But the fang blenny isn't named for its warm and fuzzy nature, or for its love of parasites and fish goobers. It rather relishes the odd scale and whatever fish snot and flesh it can tear free in a Times Square Second, before it skedaddles for cover—ARRGGGHH! Come back here ya mutt!

Leave it to a cornetfish (above) or a spotted eagle ray (next page) to restore calm . . .

Spotted eagle ray, South Maui.

Among the graceful swimmers are the triggerfish— the black durgon (left), the pinktail durgon (top right), and the gilded triggerfish (bottom right).

This is a pennant butterfly, often seen in schools but easily confused with . . .

. . . the Moorish Idol
(above).

These damsels (right)
often defend home coral
heads.

The damselfish or Hawaiian dascyllus (above), less than 5" long, is a profile in attitude. But a Potter's angel (below) is more circumspect.

Whodaguy?. . . It's a hungry unicorn. But, alas, friendly fish coming in from a distance indicate tourists with fish food in the area. Fish food kills reefs.

The yellowfin surgeon is among Neptune's beauties. *FISHWATCHER'S NOTE: The only difference between an eyestripe surgeon and yellowfin surgeon is that a yellowfin has yellow fins. These 2 species are identical, forward of the gill plates.*

Chubs are gun-metal-gray—except for their golden phase, when they dazzle the reef. This highlighter was photographed in natural light at about 4' in Ahihi Bay, South Maui.

Back on a shallower reef is where we'll likely encounter more triggerfish too.

Right is a lagoon triggerfish, also known as humuhumunukunukuapua'a.

Above is a lei triggerfish or humuhumulei. *Below: The Bouncer—"I'm sorry but you'll have to leave."*

We used to see vast schools of goatfish (*weke*—VEH-keh) in Hawaii. *No mo stay.* Maybe they'll be back, once a few wrong things are made right.

A young manybar goatfish, or moano (right), stays close to cover. Below is a whitesaddle goatfish.

Above is a blue goatfish, and below are bandtail goatfish.

I, Snorkel Bob, cruise near the top of the food chain with an eye on reef cleanliness, so this shortbody blenny femme could easily have sensed a stalker, a snacker, a gobbler of pretty young things. She froze for the shot and split in a blink as I lowered the rig to assure no dark intention. Smart girl.

The arceye hawkfish has an arc over each eye, and he perches on the coral like a hawk, watching for prey passing below. This may be the most photographed fish on the reef, because he sits still.

The filefishes are also numerous. On the right is a squaretail filefish, seen by the thousands at Molokini Crater in the '80s and '90s. This guy may indicate a return.

The barred filefish (below) has visible ribs—not really; those are not ribs but the color pattern. This fish's skin was commonly used as drumhead material in Hawaii, back in the day. Today, many barred filefish are introversive and self-conscious because of the egregious overbite, but most find a mate sooner or later.
"Oh, Spike! You want me to what?"

Goldring surgeonfish or kole (KOH-leh), like all surgeons, are herbivores vital to reef health.

The hermit crab below went nearly a foot in length. Hermit crabs are a lynchpin species on any reef but suffer massive extraction with zero management in Hawaii. Hermits change shells as they grow. When a hermit dies, he leaves a shell. 300,000 hermits leaving Oahu and the Big Island annually pose severe threats of reef collapse in those places—they wholesale for 11¢ each. Are you seeing red yet, like me, Snorkel Bob? In all my years on the reef, this is the only jumbo hermit encountered, so I dasn't say where.

Moving down to the itty bitty category,
this whip coral gobie went about ½",
though here he goes a full page.

These adorable grubs might look cute and cuddly, but many nudibranchs effuse toxins, making them more hazardous than teddy bears—or the crocodile needlefish (bottom), who looks scarier than me, Snorkel Bob, after somebody slipped me a decaf. You can't see here that an intrepid Hawaiian cleaner wrasse is working the choppers on the blindside, which will soon give rise to a bright new grin.

Speaking of flamboyance, we might as well wave the razzle dazzle wand on a few reds the reef provides, starting with a barred hawkfish (below). FISHWATCHER'S NOTE: Not all barred hawks have the dark splotch at the base of the tail. This is an adult in terminal splendor.

169

Do you have a tic tac?

Belted Wrasse

The Community in Action

Okay, maybe the title of this section could be: "Here's Where I, Snorkel Bob, Got Lucky with the Camera." Hey, I'll take it.

Humuhumlei *or lei triggerfish*

You can't really look for a baby dragon wrasse; you must keep an open mind and roll your eyeballs over each bit of frolicking flotsam. Nearly every hunt undertaken by me, Snorkel Bob, leads to something else. The dancing detritus (above) was a happy little dragon in 10' of water, once I'd given up on finding whatever it was I thought I needed.

Below: Razor Boy wonders how he got so handsome.

Inset: They're so cute at that age. Razor Baby, $^1/_2$" long.

Forceps Butterflyfish
(Lauwiliwilinukunuku'oi'oi)

Shortbodied Blenny (Tao'o kauila)

All blennies walk a fine line between stolid defense and quick flight for cover. The shortbodied blenny shown here sits firmly in defense, protecting eggs. We all strive for reef recovery, for our blenny children and our blenny children's children, so future generations of blennies can love what we have loved.

Cleaner Shrimp

Ringtail Wrasse (Po'ou)

Lest we forget: Hawaiian monk seals are endangered. 3 were murdered in 2009 in the Main Hawaiian Islands.

Thanks to Keiko Bonk and Save Our Seals, legislation may soon protect the monks and put the culprits where they belong.

photo by Dale Bonar

Very rare and most often reclusive, this obliging longnose butterfly in black paused for a profile with dorsal flair.

As noted elsewhere, the blueline butterfly seen here has been rendered gone from reefs around Hawaii. Some aquarium collectors say the blueline butterfly was never there in the first place. "Pshaw," say I, Snorkel Bob—or something to that effect.

I, Snorkel Bob, can't get enough of Cleaner Boy and his amazing antics, bringing out the performer in the most reluctant of fishes. I call this one "Cleaner Boy Wallowing in Dorsal Jams."

As noted, many thousands of featherdusters were taken from Kane'ohe Bay on Oahu for the aquarium trade by smashing the coral with a club—the featherduster is a worm burrowed into the coral with a plumage of gills for

gathering snax. Now the aquarium hunters say they don't do that anymore, yet featherdusters ship out daily, and I, Snorkel Bob, have never seen one cued up on the bottom hoping for a better life in a mainland glass cubicle. Bah!

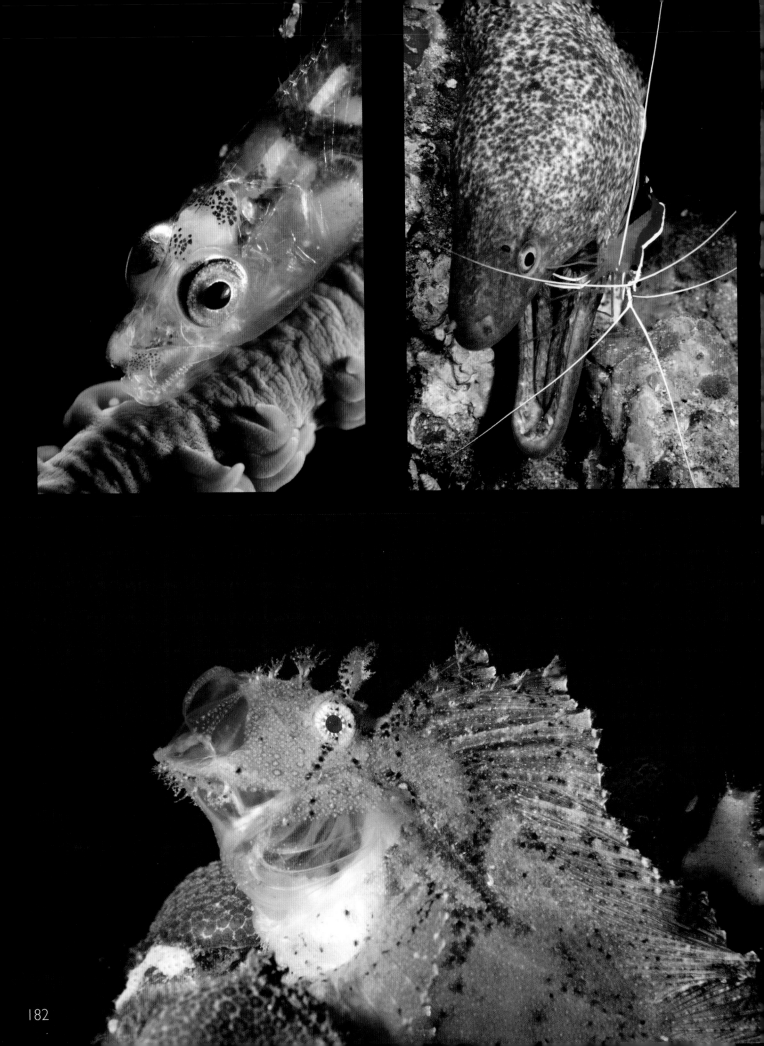

Humility

in which an international celebrity and world-renowned snorkel executive—nay, the selfsame reef icon often called The Best Snorkeler West of the Fertile Crescent—sublimely feels insignificant, next to the vast potential ahead . . .

What a hotshot u/w photog am I, Snorkel Bob! Or so I thought. Yes, even His Hugeness is humbled in the presence of such reef excellence as shown herein. I have shots from the beginning—not so long ago—that seemed great. Now I think, *Oh, brother. You call that schlock decent?*

And so I pass this way again, wondering why I bother with this fish photo razzmatazz. Of course I know why; it's because: Hot damn! This is fun!

Anyway, invitations to show *Some Fishes They Have Known* were based on personal acquaintance, technical and artistic excellence, and reef community service. The guests are:

Mike Roberts leads private u/w photo workshops (beginner to advanced) and photo dives on Maui: www.tortuga-web.com. You want to pussyfoot around or penetrate the potential? Or buy photos at www.mauireeflections.com.

Mike said, "One of the sad changes over the years is the wholesale disappearance of entire schools of a given reef species. A reef we used to call bi-color anthias rock hosted hundreds of that species for years—till one day they disappeared and have yet to return. I have no doubt that reef was emptied by aquarium fish hunters— this is such a valuable fish to that trade and easy to catch. Also disappearing fast are Potter's angels, flame angels, and yellow tangs, all aquarium favorites. We used to see yellow tangs in large schools from the beach. Now they're all but extinct on Maui. Considering the mortality of these

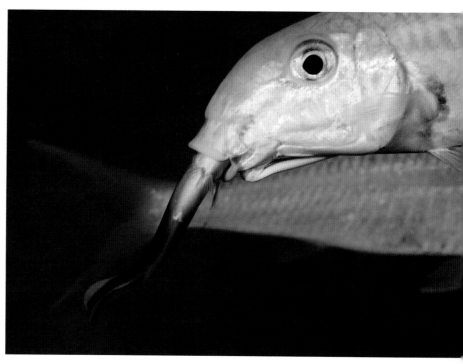

Not a goatfish eating a Hawaiian cleaner wrasse—strange but true, Cleaner Boy is snatching tonsil goobers for a grateful goat.

gathered fish and their disappearance from their natural habitat, I find it odd that those who keep saltwater tanks call themselves fish lovers. They may love to own fish but they most certainly do not love the fish."

In his u/w photog workshops, Mike Roberts also teaches reef etiquette: "If you want to capture an octopus, puff a puffer, or otherwise disrespect reef fauna, you won't be happy with me. I try to pass on what I've learned as a naturalist." Mike Roberts frequently donates photos to reef protection events, brochures, presentations, and reef info signs at many Maui beaches. He's on hand for reef cleanup and submits testimony on legislation.

Photos by Mike Roberts: Yellowstripe goatfish and Hawaiian cleaner wrasse (above). Facing page: Wirecoral goby (top left), moray eel with cleaner shrimp (top right), and leaf scorpionfish (bottom).

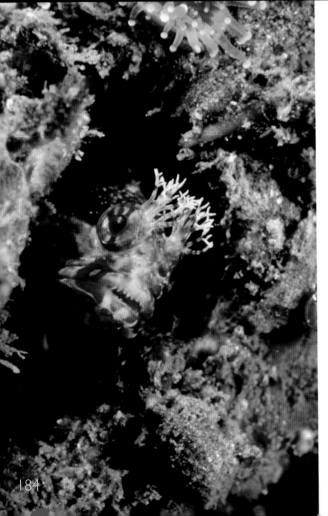

James Forte, Santa Barbara, sells underwater camera equipment at Cameras Below (www.camerasbelow.com) and marine images at www.turnerforte.com. James said, "I'll answer the phone when you call, which you'll do the first few months with tons of questions. We'll begin with a full review of your camera housing and every button and switch." Rarely is service delivered as represented, but James Forte did just that.

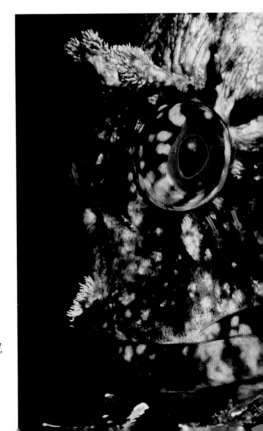

Photos by James Forte: Garibaldi, San Clemente Island, CA (top), yellowfin fringehead (left), and sculpin (right), Catalina Island, CA.

Fernando Lopez Arbarello, Maui (a.k.a. Ferrrnando!), is a Distribution Manager with Snorkel Bob's, all islands, 8–5 Every Day, including Christmas and Tu B'Shevat. To this day, divers call out: "Don't follow Fernando!" He goes over the side and down to 140' for a tiny shrimp shot, or out to eagle rays in a tide rip, or (Oy!) to the pinnacles off Black Rock alone at night to point his light nose-to-nose at a giant moray in full gape, measuring Ferrrrnando (!) for engorgement. It's www.ferlopez.com for a reef gallery of prints, downloads, fish tees, fish cards, fish tats—

like a giant squib climbing outa your skivvies (!)—I mean squid—all for sale, plus a most infinitesimal line of reef chachkas, like a B&W shot of the Wreck of the St. Anthony, fish face coffee mugs and, as you may guess, much, much more.

Jump 3 pages to 188 for *Más* Fernando!

Photos by Fernando Lopez Arbarello: Shortbodied blenny, Maui (top) and pipefish, Maui (bottom).

Octorepose

Fin . . .

Which is not to say the end but until next time—*a hui hou*. Some say the world can't survive without reefs. What a grim prospect if it could. Underwater is under the radar on crimes against nature. If a few reef-minded people cannot stop a few greedy people, the reefs will die. Stand up. Step up. Speak up, like Ronald Reagan, President of the United States of America, when he said: "Mr. Gorbachev! Tear *down* this aquarium!"

But Snorkel Bob, you ask. Who do I stand up, step up, and speak to?

Listen: I met a fisherman who was running for governor. I told him I never heard of him but would vote for him, and I did. He later told me that people were upset that I didn't want them eating fish. I never said that. But perception is reality, he said. I said okay, maybe nobody should eat fish for a while. Catfish maybe, or freshwater eels—but not ocean fish.

Another woman told me that in her *ahapua'a* you must eat fish to qualify for fishery management. I told her that's hokum. I, Snorkel Bob, don't have to eat anything.

Another woman told me about a street guy in Kona, a demented dirtball who finally disappeared. Meanwhile, he begged money or part of your sandwich, muttering, "It's time to leave the fish alone." He was laughable, so unhinged. My friend laughed, telling the story. "You remind me of that guy," she said. I dribbled my beer to enhance the picture of the nutty guy who summarized my feelings.

"It's time to leave the fish alone," I told her. It's time to leave the fish alone.

The Big Commercial Fishing lobby now blocks ocean recovery in Hawaii. BCF stonewalls all regulation on ocean extraction, because BCF is Big Money. BCF caters fundraisers for political mechanics with no vision, no plan. All ocean conservation bills must pass through the Water and Land Committees in both the Senate and the House, where every conservation bill in recent years has died—or been killed—by politics as usual with a dose of cyanide. These old power brokers will fade, and Hawaii will soon get a new governor and new committee chairs. BCF will still pursue the last fish, and if BCF lobbyists prevail, the reefs will perish.

I met personally with ¾ of the legislature and found clear consensus for reef recovery. But a back scratch longstanding hamstrings the distinguished few. So we wait for vision and a plan and the backbone to fix the sorry state of affairs in the State of Hawaii. We wait to displace greed and power brokerage in the Governor's mansion and the Legislature. Maybe a gay Republican or an evangelical Scientologist, a real Democrat or a transvestite transsexual from Transylvania will stand up to BCF, so Hawaii reefs may survive.

What can you do? Don't buy fish, for starters—or cut way back. The Western Pacific Regional Fisheries Management Council (WESPAC) came under Federal investigation for conflict of interest, campaigning with BCF for more fish with more turtle kills, as the aquarium guys cry out that their catch is declining. Duh. Hawaii reefs are weakening, as BCF supports a few greedy aquarium catchers who decimate fish species and ransack a billion-dollar tourism industry.

The dots are connected. Will you watch? Or speak up?

Más Fernando!

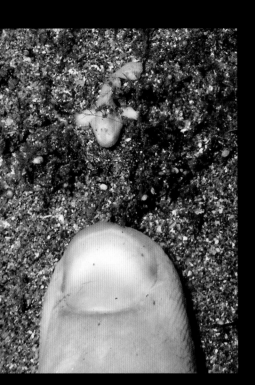

These photos by Fernando Lopez Arbarello reflect the waterman by showing what the reef revealed to him.

I saw a yellow dot and realized that it actually had shape—a baby frogfish, sitting in the sand near a reef (left).

This tiny neon cleaner wrasse was working on some fish at Five Graves, so I got in line to wait my turn. It took a while for Tiny Tim to gain confidence and grant my request, but then he cleaned my hand. Yummy. I loved him, too (right).

I saw a big cornet working Ulua reef when I was charged by this tiny Hawaiian lionfish (below), who thought my black wetsuit was a cave opening. I offered my hand, and he took cover. The cornet split. After this photo op, I found a little reef puka with no octopus, eel, or crab. Tiny lion saw the all-clear and flapped his tiny wings with a look back—"Thanks, Fernando! And hey, send me a copy, okay?"

Si, mi pequeño amigo, *here you go—and hey, yourself! Watch out for the aquarium* bandidos!

INDEX

Only I, Snorkel Bob, manufacture masks, fins, and snorkels in kid format to world-class specs, including Rx lenses for your 4-eyed jr. barracuda, because reef love is for life—I, Snorkel Bob, do this for the fish, so the children can open their eyes and see what is theirs to protect. Is your child unusual? Put her in the water. See what she can do.

The Hawaii aquarium trade is unchecked, desecrating Hawaii reefs to fill 80% of US aquaria. 99% die within a year of capture, said a Kona aquarium guru, but they are the "livestock necessary" to drive hardware sales. Many die in transit. Those fish live up to 40 years on the reef—yellow tangs eating algae, Hawaiian cleaner wrasses controlling parasites. Yet they leave $3–4 in Hawaii on their way to retail at $40–$50 on the mainland.

Toby Girl at home in Hawaii.

Hawaii aquarium hunters have no catch limit, no limit on the number of catchers, and no constraint on species. 60% of the aquarium catch are herbivores, compounding a major threat to Hawaii reefs. A reef system cannot survive without habitat and species.

If you see these fish in waiting rooms, bistros, hotels, or anywhere: stand up.

Step up and speak up—in the spirit of Ronald Reagan call out:

"Mr. Gorbachev, tear *down* this aquarium!"

If the tank is a commercial rental, advise them to UNSUBSCRIBE. If it's a private tank, let the fish live out their lives and THEN take it down.

Go to www.snorkelbob.com with proof positive for each aquarium successfully removed from this system and score a point for every gallon. Points translate to discounts and premiums on a life of reef love.

SNORKEL BOB, himself, is a waterlogged, gill-breathing, fin-scratching reef addict. Above mean high water he's immersed in that least destructive of human behaviors, the pursuit of art. Under the *nom de plume (et la guerre)* of Robert Wintner, he has served a humble offering of literary fiction to mixed reviews—raves from the literarily astute; ravings from the values-challenged.

Stay tuned. Coming up:
Every Fish Tells a Story.

Photo by Fernando Lopez Arbarello, who missed the frontal shot and scrambled to salvage the walkaway of a 3some common to frogfish, with her in the center leading 2 consorts by the pectoral fins.

A hui hou